Differentiating
School
Leadership

*To every principal who is willing and able to adjust
their leadership to meet the challenges of a new situation.*

Differentiating
School
Leadership
Facing the Challenges
of Practice

Daniel L. Duke

CORWIN
A SAGE Company

For information:

Corwin
A SAGE Company
2455 Teller Road
Thousand Oaks, California 91320
(800) 233-9936
Fax: (800) 417-2466
www.corwinpress.com

SAGE India Pvt. Ltd.
B 1/I 1 Mohan Cooperative
   Industrial Area
Mathura Road, New Delhi 110 044
India

SAGE Ltd.
1 Oliver's Yard
55 City Road
London EC1Y 1SP
United Kingdom

SAGE Asia-Pacific Pte. Ltd.
33 Pekin Street #02-01
Far East Square
Singapore 048763

Printed in the United States of America

Library of Congress Cataloging-in-Publication Data

Duke, Daniel Linden.
Differentiating school leadership: facing the challenges of practice/Daniel L. Duke.
      p. cm.
Includes bibliographical references and index.
ISBN 978-1-4129-7050-1 (pbk.)
    1. School principals—Attitudes. 2. School principals—In-service training.
3. Educational leadership. 4. Educational accountability. 5. Educational productivity.
I. Title.

LB2831.9.D84 2010
371.2'012—dc22   2009031807

This book is printed on acid-free paper.

09   10   11   12   13   10   9   8   7   6   5   4   3   2   1

Acquisitions Editor:	Arnis Burvikovs
Associate Editor:	Desirée A. Bartlett
Production Editor:	Libby Larson
Copy Editor:	Jeannette McCoy
Typesetter:	C&M Digitals (P) Ltd.
Proofreader:	Theresa Kay
Indexer:	Ellen Slavitz
Cover Designer:	Scott Van Atta

Contents

Acknowledgments

Corwin gratefully acknowledges the contributions of the following individuals:

Kenneth Austin, Assistant Professor
Department of Secondary Education and Educational Leadership
Stephen F. Austin State University
Nacogdoches, TX

Jacie Bejster-Maslyk, Principal
Crafton Elementary School
Carlynton School District
Pittsburgh, PA

Dan W. Butin, Assistant Dean
Department of Educational Leadership
School of Education, Cambridge College
Cambridge, MA

Michelle Gayle, Principal
Griffin Middle School
Tallahassee, FL

Sandra Harris, Professor, Director
Center for Research and Doctoral Studies
Department of Educational Leadership
Lamar University
Beaumont, TX

Stephen Shepperd, Retired Elementary Principal
Kellogg, ID

Kim Vogel, Principal
Parkdale Elementary School
Parkdale, OR

About the Author

After teaching high school social studies and serving as a secondary school administrator, **Daniel L. Duke** embarked on a career in higher education. For over three decades he has taught courses on educational leadership, organizational change, and school reform as well as conducting research on various aspects of public schools. After serving on the faculties of Lewis and Clark College and Stanford University, he came to the University of Virginia as Chair of Educational Leadership and Policy Studies. He founded and directed the Thomas Jefferson Center for Educational Design and helped establish the Darden-Curry Partnership for Leaders in Education (PLE), a unique enterprise involving the Curry School of Education and the Darden Graduate School of Business Administration. He serves as Research Director for the PLE. A prolific writer, Duke has authored or coauthored 27 books and several hundred scholarly articles, monographs, chapters, and reports. His most recent books include *The Challenges of Educational Change* (2004), *Education Empire: The Evolution of an Excellent Suburban School System* (2005), *Teachers' Guide to School Turnarounds* (2007), and *The Little School System That Could: Transforming a City School District* (2008). A highly regarded consultant, Duke has worked with over 150 school systems, state agencies, foundations, and governments across the United States and abroad. He has served as president of the University Council for Educational Administration and was chosen as Professor of the Year at the Curry School of Education.

Introduction

All schools need leadership. This is not the issue. The issue is this—Do all schools need the same kind of leadership?

Once upon a time the primary distinction made by experts on the principalship was between management and leadership. Principals were exhorted to function less like managers and more like leaders (Duke, 1987). What it meant to function like a leader, however, varied greatly from one expert to the next. No one today maintains that all school principals exercise leadership in the same way. Some principals, in fact, are not perceived to exercise leadership at all. The question is—*Should* all principals exercise leadership in the same way?

A number of experts on school leadership write as if there is one best way to lead a school, regardless of the type of school or the challenges it faces. These individuals frequently place an adjective in front of leadership to capture the type of leadership they advocate. Instructional leadership. Democratic leadership. Moral leadership. Transformational leadership. Servant leadership. There is no lack of opinions when it comes to prescribing the best way to lead schools.

Reeves (2006) adopts a variation on this theme. Instead of advocating one superior type of leadership, he identifies different "dimensions" of leadership. Each dimension represents a different realm of responsibility, and each calls for leadership. Among the dimensions are visionary leadership, relational leadership, systems leadership, reflective leadership, collaborative leadership, and communicative leadership. Presumably effective leaders need to exercise leadership in all, or at least most, of these dimensions.

In this book, I opt for a position somewhat different from the ones held by many of my colleagues. For almost four decades, I have worked in schools, conducted research on schools, and consulted with schools. I have seen high-performing schools and low-performing schools, schools faced with the need to change rapidly and schools desperately trying to preserve their culture and identity, schools in troubled neighborhoods and schools in idyllic suburbs. In all honesty, I have not found that there is one best way to lead all of these schools. Having said this, I also must add that some ways of leading clearly are more appropriate for certain circumstances than other ways of leading.

The past decade has witnessed growing recognition that there is not one best way to teach all students. My colleague Carol Ann Tomlinson and dozens of other experts have made a strong case for differentiating instruction based on the needs, interests, prior learning, and abilities of learners. I make a similar case in this book for differentiating leadership. Schools function in different contexts and face different challenges. These differences call for school leaders to differentiate their priorities, theories of action, and ways of leading. There is no compelling evidence that generic leadership of any type works well under all circumstances.

In this book you will be introduced to some actual principals and the different circumstances that they confronted. One faced the possibility of declining student achievement that attended the arrival of large numbers of English language learners. Another was charged with turning around a low-performing school. A third principal had to address the challenge of sustaining school improvements beyond impressive initial success. Three other principals dealt with the challenge of developing innovative new schools from scratch. In order to address each of these distinctive challenges effectively, the principals needed to decide where and how to focus the limited resources available to them. The essence of differentiating school leadership is to be found in the priorities identified for particular circumstances. Effective leadership is impossible when everything is considered a high priority. Table 0.1 provides an overview of the four challenges discussed in this book and the priorities associated with each one.

Table 0.1   Different Challenges, Different Priorities

Preventing school decline	Determine needs of new students Assess school's capacity to meet needs
Turning around a low-performing school	Focus on literacy, math, and discipline Achieve "quick wins" to boost confidence Cultivate teacher teams
Sustaining school improvements	Strengthen curriculum beyond literacy and math Develop a continuum of interventions Work on school reculturing
Designing an innovative school	Challenge assumptions about learning and teaching Examine a wide range of program options Mobilize broad-based support

SUPPORT FOR THE IDEA OF DIFFERENTIATING LEADERSHIP

That different circumstances call for different leadership is hardly a new idea. Organization theorists working primarily on the challenges of leading private businesses and military organizations began to stress the need for a differentiated view of leadership in the sixties.

Contingency theory. One of the first efforts to understand how leadership varies across different situations involved the study of military officers (Fiedler, 1964, 1967). Fiedler observed effective and ineffective leaders. He noted that the leadership style of effective leaders differed somewhat depending on the characteristics of the particular situation. Three characteristics, or what researchers call *situational variables,* were of particular importance: leader-member relations, task structure, and position power.

Leader-member relations are determined by how organization members feel about a leader. Do they trust the leader? Are they confident that the leader can accomplish the mission? Are they prepared to support the leader? When leaders enjoy positive relations with subordinates, they are much more likely to be effective. Under certain circumstances, however, leaders must proceed in the absence of positive relations.

Task structure, the second situational variable, involves the clarity of the task at hand. Fiedler found that tasks that were highly structured and clearly defined were associated with a greater level of control by the leader. Tasks that were vague and unclear, on the other hand, made it more difficult for leaders to exercise control. When a task is highly structured, people understand what needs to be done in order to complete the task and what they individually are expected to contribute to the undertaking. This high level of awareness presumably makes them more likely to follow directions and accept the leader's influence. Uncertainty regarding what must be accomplished and how it should be accomplished can cause followers to question leadership.

Position power concerns a leader's authority to reward and punish the actions of followers. A high level of position power is represented by the ability to control pay, incentives, and employment status. Without such control, leaders are at a disadvantage when trying to influence the conduct of followers.

Using the three situational variables, Fiedler (1964, 1967) defined a favorable situation as one in which leader-member relations were positive, the task was clearly defined, and the leader enjoyed strong position power. An unfavorable situation was characterized by negative leader-member relations, an unclear task structure, and relatively modest position power. Fiedler conducted research to determine whether one particular style of leadership was better suited to one situation than the other. He found that leaders with a high level of motivation to accomplish a task were more effective in both the highly favorable and the highly unfavorable situations described above. Leaders who focused more on the quality of relations with followers were found to be more effective in situations that fell between the two extremes (e.g., where one of the situational variables was positive and the other two were negative). Fiedler failed, though, to provide an adequate explanation for these somewhat curious findings (Northouse, 2007, pp. 115–116).

Situational leadership. Around the same time that Fiedler was developing his contingency model, Hersey and Blanchard (1969) published a model that came to be known as *situational leadership.* Somewhat simpler than Fiedler's model, situational leadership involves two basic dimensions that, when combined, create the possibility of four relatively distinct leadership styles. The two dimensions are both related to subordinates' level of development.

The first dimension concerns subordinates' need for direction. Presumably employees in some situations require a greater amount of leader direction than employees in other situations. The second dimension concerns the need for support. Followers require a greater level of leader support under certain circumstances than others. Hersey and Blanchard used the two dimensions to propose four leadership styles.

A high supportive and low directive style of leadership is suited to situations in which subordinates are capable of assuming responsibility for day-to-day decisions. Rather than closely supervising employee behavior, the leader can be guided by the advice and concerns of employees. The leader focuses on providing helpful feedback and encouragement.

A high supportive and high directive style of leadership is called for when subordinates' efforts need to be focused on achieving specific goals according to relatively precise guidelines. Subordinates' input, once again, is highly valued. The leader must be sensitive to the needs of employees and provide ample feedback and encouragement.

The third leadership style is high directive and low supportive. The leader's interactions with subordinates focus on accomplishing specific goals, many of which may not be inherently interesting to subordinates. Less time is spent on providing support and encouragement. Situations that call for this style of leadership are perceived to necessitate close supervision.

A low supportive and low directive leadership style constitutes Hersey and Blanchard's (1969) fourth option. The leader's involvement in supervising goal-oriented effort and providing emotional support is relatively small. Subordinates are presumed to be capable of assuming a substantial degree of responsibility for accomplishing the work at hand and supporting each other in the process.

The strength of situational leadership is also its weakness. While simple and easy to understand, the model is hard to apply to complex situations characterized by varying levels of employee commitment and competence. The situational leadership model was developed deductively, and relatively little research has been conducted to test the model under actual organizational circumstances. Northouse (2007, p. 99) also notes that Hersey and Blanchard fail to address the issue of one-to-one versus group leadership. Should leaders, in other words, focus on matching their style to each individual employee or to groups of employees?

Despite these and other shortcomings, the situational leadership model has the benefit of recognizing that leaders confront varying circumstances that are likely to require different combinations of skills.

Path-goal theory. A third approach to leadership that recognizes the need for differentiation is path-goal theory (House, 1971). Whereas situational leadership requires leaders to take into account the developmental level of subordinates, path-goal theory calls for a match of leadership style to characteristics of the work setting as well as characteristics of subordinates. A key assumption of path-goal theory is that the motivation of subordinates can vary with the tasks to be accomplished and the nature of the work environment. It is the leader's responsibility to assess employee motivation and choose a leadership style that is likely to promote a high level of motivation, given certain characteristics of the work environment. Leaders may need to remove obstacles that prevent employees from accomplishing their goals, offer incentives to encourage employees, and ensure that employees find their work meaningful.

Four leadership styles emerge from path-goal theory. Directive leadership calls for close supervision of work and the provision of explicit guidance concerning how work is to be done. It is most appropriate when employees are dogmatic and the tasks to be accomplished are ambiguous and complex. Supportive leadership requires leaders to relate to employees in a nurturing manner. Work environments characterized by repetitive and unchallenging tasks and employees who are unsatisfied and in need of affiliation benefit from supportive leadership, according to path-goal theory.

Participative leadership, the third style, focuses on involving employees in decision making. It is best suited to situations in which tasks are unclear and unstructured and employees are capable of functioning autonomously. The last leadership style, achievement-oriented leadership, addresses employees' need to be challenged. Work environments characterized by tasks that are difficult and employees who need to perform at high levels call for achievement-oriented leadership.

One strength of path-goal theory is its focus on having leaders do what is necessary to assist subordinates in accomplishing what they are expected to accomplish. The theory also recognizes that all employees may not share the same level of motivation. The theory unfortunately offers little guidance to leaders about what to do when employees are characterized by varying levels of motivation. Adjusting leadership style to individual employees in the same organization may seem logical in theory, but in practice, such an approach can be challenging. Leaders who treat employees differently are open to accusations of discrimination and favoritism.

Recent work on leadership. In the decades since the development of contingency theory, situational leadership, and path-goal theory, interest in differentiating leadership has continued to grow. In one of the more popular approaches, an effort is made to match leadership style with the emotional needs of different groups (Goleman, Boyatzis, & McKee, 2002). Six leadership styles are identified, each linked to a particular emotional climate.

Visionary leadership, for example, helps people in need of an inspiring new direction in their life or work. When individuals need to improve performance, coaching leadership is suited to building their long-term capabilities. Affilative leadership addresses situations in which rifts among group members need to be healed and cooperation promoted. Achieving consensus and eliciting buy in for new initiatives is the primary focus of democratic leadership. When groups are expected to produce high-quality results and achieve ambitious goals, pacesetting leadership is recommended. Commanding leadership is called for when a crisis looms or a quick turnaround in performance is necessitated.

None of the work cited so far was undertaken with school leaders in mind. This gap has begun to be addressed by Kise and Russell (2008) in *Differentiated School Leadership: Effective Collaboration, Communication, and Change Through Personality Type.* The authors recognize the value of understanding different personality types when adopting a leadership style. Such knowledge can be used to promote effective teamwork in schools and foster leadership at all levels of school operations.

BEGINNING WITH THE SITUATION, NOT THE LEADERSHIP STYLE

All of the work mentioned above contributes greatly to making the case that one type of leadership is not universally appropriate. For the most part, though, these theories and models begin with the identification of leadership styles. With the exception of Fiedler's early work, the leadership styles were developed deductively and then matched to the presumed requirements of hypothetical situations.

The approach taken in this book is somewhat different. It is not a style-based approach. The starting points for inquiry are actual situations facing contemporary school principals. Spillane (2005), in writing about distributed leadership, notes, "The situation both enables and constrains leadership practice." He goes on to point out that aspects of "the situation define and are defined by leadership practice in interaction with leaders and followers" (p. 147). Drawing on published and unpublished accounts of different leadership situations as well as empirical research on school leadership, key functions associated with leadership for particular situations are identified. All principals, of course, must possess a wide range of skills and knowledge. Depending on the situation, however, certain skills and knowledge may be especially important. Knowing what to focus on and when to focus on it can spell the difference between success and failure. Principals are likely to experience serious problems when they fail to appreciate the special qualities of a situation and the kinds of leadership actions that it calls for.

There are potentially a variety of ways to characterize a school "situation." Situations may be distinguished by the level of the school (elementary, middle, high), the size of the school, the school program (college preparatory, vocational-technical, alternative), and the location of the school (urban, suburban, rural). While each of these variations may necessitate adjustments in leadership, they will not be the foci of discussion in this book. *Differentiating School Leadership* concentrates on four challenges that are sufficiently distinct to call for different sets of organizational priorities. No claim is made, of course, that these are the only challenges to call for different approaches by principals.

The first challenge to be addressed in this book involves the prospect of school decline. No school is exempt from the possibility of falling performance. Every principal knows that any success his or her school currently is experiencing may be jeopardized by a variety of factors: an unexpected influx of at-risk students, a larger-than-anticipated drop in revenue, new state and federal mandates, a large turnover in key personnel. While some principals are able to negotiate such straits, others flounder. Their schools enter a downward spiral where each poor judgment and inadequate response serves to accelerate the negative impact on teaching and learning. Part I of this book examines what principals can do to confront a challenge to school performance and prevent sustained decline.

Part II is devoted to a second set of circumstances, one involving a school that is consistently low performing. In this era of educational accountability, such schools must be turned around, or they face a series of sanctions that eventually can lead to reconstitution or closure. What must a principal focus on in order to affect a dramatic increase in student achievement? Studies of successful school turnarounds are yielding a wealth of data on the specific steps that principals need to take in order to address academic problems and improve instruction quickly.

Achieving a turnaround is one thing; sustaining it can be quite a different matter. The history of educational reform is littered with examples of promising changes that failed to become institutionalized. Understanding why so many reforms are short-lived is one key to sustaining school improvements. Part III investigates what it takes to lead improving schools so that momentum is not lost over time. Key elements of such leadership include strengthening the entire academic program, expanding the school's capacity to help students, and reculturing the school.

Part IV concerns the challenge of designing a school from scratch and then bringing the school to life. The leaders on which Chapter 7 focuses were especially interested in developing new models for learning and teaching. They were willing to challenge prevailing assumptions about schooling and explore a range of possibilities. Once they had completed the design process, they also were able to mobilize the support necessary to open their schools.

These four challenging situations, of course, barely scratch the surface of possibilities. One can imagine the leadership needed to close a well-established school or move a school from "good to great." The kind of leadership needed to run a successful charter school is likely to be quite different from that required in many regular school settings. Leading a school in the aftermath of a disaster such as Hurricane Katrina presents unique challenges. So too does leading a nonpublic school that depends on tuitions and donations. Putting the four previously mentioned situations under the microscope, however, should be sufficient to illustrate the fact that school leadership is not a "one-size-fits-all" proposition.

The book concludes with two chapters that address some lessons on leadership. Chapter 8 departs from the preceding discussions of how school leaders succeed when faced with qualitatively different challenges. Instead, the focus is the various ways that school leaders can undermine their own effectiveness. The possible mistakes range from misdiagnosing the cause of school problems to failing to follow up and follow through. Chapter 9 considers the implications of differentiating school leadership for the preparation, selection, evaluation, and study of school leaders.

TIME AND FOCUS

One of the guiding assumptions for this book is the fact that virtually all principals have more to do than time available to do it. It does not matter whether the principal heads a small elementary school or a huge comprehensive high school. Principals must constantly live with the realization that there is always another phone call that needs to be made, another classroom that should be visited, and another student or teacher who could have benefited from a brief conversation.

Nearly a quarter century ago in another book on school leadership, I wondered why some principals were more effective than others, when few, if any, principals accomplished everything they needed or were expected to do (Duke, 1987). While I am still wondering about this perplexing matter, I am confident that two keys to differential effectiveness among principals involve (a) their ability to focus and (b) what they choose to focus on.

Some principals, it seems, are incapable of zeroing in on a set of priorities. Why this should be the case is debatable. Perhaps they lack a vision of what an effective school should look like, a vision that can guide them during times of confusion and conflict. Perhaps they dislike telling people that they cannot have what they want under a particular set of circumstances. Or perhaps they naively assume that careful planning and a high level of commitment from the staff are sufficient to enable a school to address a lengthy list of concerns simultaneously. Whatever the reason, the schools led by these principals are places where people often are unsure about which functions are most important for achieving their mission. Clear direction from the top is missing, and staff members are left to wonder about how best to allocate their limited time and energy.

Other principals manifest a keen understanding of the need for priorities. They recognize time and energy are scarce resources that need to be focused. Unfortunately, these principals choose to focus on the wrong priorities. They may decide, for example, to launch a major public relations campaign in order to win the support of parents and community members. It would have been better, though, to concentrate on improving instruction in reading, thereby helping students to raise their academic performance. When students do well academically, there is little need for elaborate public relations initiatives.

Determining where to focus time and energy is a matter of *organizational diagnostics*. Organizational diagnostics encompass the processes by which organization leaders assess the impediments that stand between them and the achievement of their organizations' missions. Some of these impediments derive from the environments in which schools operate. Schools cannot be separated from their contexts. Every context is characterized by challenges. Challenges also can arise within schools. Schools, in other words, can generate their own impediments. The four challenges in this book—avoiding school decline, achieving school turnaround, sustaining school improvement, and creating a new school—entail both environmental and internal components.

Once principals diagnose the nature of the challenge or challenges that need to be addressed, they must decide where and how to focus their own limited time and energy and that of their staffs. Arriving at decisions regarding organizational focus is the primary work of school leaders. Individual staff members may be unwilling or unable to see beyond the needs of their particular unit or program. Principals, however, are positioned to look across all units and programs in order to consider the mission and welfare of the entire school. Determining what must be done to address particular challenges calls for the careful collection and assessment of various types of data—data on past and present student performance, data on the quality of teaching, data on school attendance and student behavior, data on curriculum alignment, data on program effectiveness, and so on. The primary purpose of this book is to help school leaders and those who aspire to school leadership to diagnose different challenges and determine how best to focus efforts in order to respond to these challenges successfully.

PART I

The Challenge of School Decline

Every principal fears that he or she may be confronted with circumstances that can lead to school decline. No educational leader wants to have student achievement and a school's hard-earned reputation plummet during his or her watch. This section looks at the conditions that can cause academic performance to drop and the leadership needed to prevent it. Being able to recognize the signs of incipient decline obviously is an important part of the process. Among the potential causes of school decline are shifts in the makeup of the student body, budget cuts, and changes in school culture. To the public, however, blame for school decline is often attributed to principals' failure to address these challenges effectively.

1

Recognizing the Potential for School Decline

A SCHOOL ON THE BRINK*

Eli Buck reflected back on what might have been. Waverly Elementary School entered the 21st century as one of Westville's premier elementary schools, but just how long its reputation could be maintained was open to considerable local conjecture. Since the late 1990s, the Hispanic population of Westville had steadily climbed. The region once welcomed the children of middle-class immigrants, but times had changed. Increasingly, those who came from beyond U.S. borders were poor and not well educated. Many were illiterate in their native language.

Some longtime residents of Westville worried that the influx of immigrants would tax the school system and other public services, eventually leading to an exodus of longtime residents and a loss of property value. At one point in 2005, Westville gained national notoriety when the city council passed an ordinance to prevent "overcrowding" of local residences. The measure clearly was intended to curtail Hispanic residents from housing

---

*The author is indebted to Dr. Jeff Carroll and Michael J. Salmonowicz for much of the information on which the Waverly Elementary School case was based. Waverly Elementary is a pseudonym, as is the name of the principal, Eli Buck.

extended family members and unrelated "guests." Faced with threats of lawsuits from the American Civil Liberties Union and other organizations, the city council eventually backed off strict enforcement of the ordinance, but the message had been communicated. The welcome mat was not out for poor immigrants in Westville.

It did not take Eli Buck long to realize the high level of concern in the community. Soon after he became principal in June of 2004, he adjusted the marquee in front of Waverly Elementary so that messages were posted in English and Spanish. The complaints from concerned citizens were so vociferous that he felt compelled to return to English-only messages.

Several members of Buck's faculty also registered their concerns about Waverly's "changing demographics." Several veteran teachers made it clear that they had no intention of modifying their instructional practices to accommodate immigrant students. Most of Waverly's 50 teachers, however, seemed willing to do what they could to adjust to the new students, but they acknowledged their lack of adequate training. The Waverly faculty had received no site-based professional development for the previous five years. Many of the teachers had taught at Waverly for 10 or more years, well before the dramatic increase in non-English-speaking students. Teachers expressed frustration at the difficulty of communicating with parents who spoke little or no English.

Table 1.1 indicates the extent to which Waverly had become a school with a diverse student population. Not surprisingly, the percentage of students on free and reduced-price lunch had increased along with the percentage of Hispanic students. By 2004, over one-third of the students came from low-income families. When Buck took over as principal, the upper grades still were predominantly non-Hispanic, but the lower grades already consisted primarily of Hispanic students.

Table 1.1   Student Demographics, 1999–2004

	Asian	African American	Hispanic	White	Total Enrollment	Free and Reduced-Price Lunch	ESOL
Fall 1999	47	88	81	502	718[a]	100	NA
Fall 2000	44	93	105	401	643	124	84
Fall 2001	39	92	133	379	645[b]	122	144
Fall 2002	31	79	176	337	623	131	172
Fall 2003	29	93	212	297	632[b]	237	223
Fall 2004	30	81	290	287	688	230	316

NOTE: ESOL = English for speakers of other languages.

a. Includes sixth grade. School became K–5 beginning in Fall 2000.

b. Native Americans are included in Total Enrollment

Buck could see the challenge before him when he examined the passing rates on state tests in reading/language arts, mathematics, social science/history, and science. Tables 1.2 and 1.3 contain the test data for third and fifth grades. A gap in passing rates between white and Hispanic

Table 1.2   Percentage of Students Passing State Tests in Adequate Yearly Progress Categories, 2003–2004; Third Grade

	Reading/ Language Arts	Mathematics	Social Science/ History	Science
1. All students	69	85	92	91
2a. Hispanic	65	82	90	90
2b. White	74	92	92	94
2c. Asian	NA	100	NA	NA
2d. African American	68	74	100	86
3. Economically disadvantaged	55	76	76	100
4. Disabled	26	64	65	74
5. Limited-English proficiency	59	78	68	68

Table 1.3   Percentage of Students Passing State Tests in Adequate Yearly Progress Categories, 2003–2004; Fifth Grade

	Reading/ Language Arts	Mathematics	Social Science/ History	Science
1. All students	91	94	98	94
2a. Hispanic	78	85	84	78
2b. White	99	100	100	99
2c. Asian	100	100	100	100
2d. African American	84	76	100	92
3. Economically disadvantaged	81	89	90	79
4. Disabled	90	92	100	100
5. Limited-English proficiency	80	87	84	78

third graders was evident, but what really troubled Buck was the fact that the gap widened for fifth graders. In other words, the longer Hispanic (and African American) students remained at Waverly, the less well they achieved relative to white students. Buck wondered what was happening at his school to contribute to the widening achievement gap.

In addition to needing to address the daunting challenge of narrowing the achievement gap between white and minority students, Buck faced a bevy of practical problems. His school, for example, lacked sufficient instructional space to house the growing number of Title I and English as a second language (ESL) teachers. Another concern involved the practice of retaining at grade level low-achieving students. Some of Waverly's teachers strongly favored retention, but Buck understood that the effectiveness of this practice was questionable. This difference of opinion reflected a third issue. Buck believed that teachers should play an active role in school-based decision making. Knowing, however, that many members of his faculty held positions in opposition to his own beliefs, he wondered if he could afford to invite teacher participation in decision making. For their part, many teachers seemed reluctant to assume a leadership role in their grade level or at the school. Buck's predecessor had done little to nurture shared decision making.

Of all the tough issues facing Buck, however, perhaps the toughest involved the parents of his white students. Many of these parents were clearly alarmed that their children were no longer in the majority in lower-grade classrooms. They bluntly asked Buck why they shouldn't withdraw their children and move to a less diverse school.

DETECTING VULNERABILITIES

Every principal, like every physician, must be a good diagnostician in order to be effective. Good diagnosticians look at a range of conditions, not just the immediate problems that are presented to them. The challenges facing principals in the 21st century are likely to have organizational, social, political, legal, interpersonal, economic, and cultural, as well as educational, dimensions. The likelihood of addressing a challenge successfully is reduced when particular dimensions are overlooked.

The central challenge that confronted Eli Buck involved the fear that his school was poised on the brink of decline. *Decline*, in this case, refers to lower academic performance as indicated by falling passing rates on state standardized tests. Students of school decline understand that the process can be triggered by a variety of factors. In Eli Buck's case, the potential precipitant was an influx of Hispanic students with serious educational needs. Other "triggers" to school decline include inadequate funding, weak leadership, and changes in school culture. These challenges will be addressed later in the chapter.

The consequences of failure to address the prospect of lower academic achievement can be very serious. Some have characterized the result of such failure as a downward spiral in which the rate of decline steadily accelerates (Duke, 2008a). Falling test scores, for instance, can lead to parental concerns, which in turn can cause some parents to withdraw their children and send them to other schools. The consequence is a loss of resources that can lead to a reduction in staff. If the students who are withdrawn tend to be higher achieving students, then the concentration of lower achieving students grows, thereby increasing the workload for the remaining teachers and the likelihood of a continuing drop in academic achievement. Such circumstances are likely to cause plummeting teacher morale and a voluntary exodus of additional staff. Recruiting new teachers to fill openings is certain to be difficult, adding to the prospect of sustained school decline.

Whether Eli Buck foresaw all of these possibilities or not is unclear, but he clearly grasped the fact that the challenge facing him was multidimensional. Among the factors he realized could contribute to Waverly's decline if they went unaddressed were the following:

- Lack of instruction geared to the needs of newcomer students
- Overreliance on retention as an intervention
- Reluctance of teachers to assume leadership roles
- Concerns among white parents
- Difficulties concerning home-school communications with Hispanic families

Buck did not blame teachers for lacking the skills to teach students with limited ability in English. Waverly, after all, had lacked any kind of professional development aligned to the needs of its new students. What really concerned Buck, however, was the unwillingness of some teachers to embrace the need for changes in their instructional practice. In certain cases, veteran teachers who had experienced great success in the past remained convinced that their approach to teaching was appropriate for all students. They expected new students to make the adjustment to their instruction, not the reverse. Buck wanted to point out that much of these teachers' prior success could be attributed to *who* their students were, not *how* they taught.

Some teachers even felt it was not their responsibility to teach the new students. That was what Title I and ESL teachers were expected to do. Relying on pull-out programs, Buck knew, had its downside. When students left class to get help from specialists, they ran the risk of falling further behind their classmates. Prolonged absence virtually ensured that these students would never catch up. Over time, students who were retained in elementary school were more likely to have problems in middle school and eventually drop out of high school. Buck also realized, though, that promoting low achievers to the next grade was unlikely to be successful if their teachers lacked the skills to address these students' learning needs.

Given the large number of veteran teachers at Waverly and Buck's belief in teacher leadership, he wanted to enlist faculty members in the effort to avoid school decline. No principal by himself or herself can handle all the changes required to accommodate an increasingly diverse student body. Teamwork was the key, but Buck discovered that most Waverly teachers were reluctant to serve as team leaders or assume other leadership roles.

The last two factors that had to be addressed if school decline was to be averted involved Waverly's parents. White parents needed reassurance that efforts to respond to increasing student diversity would not result in their children's education being compromised. Fearing that Waverly teachers would have to spend most of their time with non-English-speaking and limited-English-speaking students, white parents threatened to send their children to other schools. Buck knew that "white flight," if it did occur, would not serve the academic interests of the students who remained at Waverly.

The other group of parents whose concerns had to be addressed was Hispanic parents, but the language barrier presented a formidable obstacle. There were few Spanish-speaking staff members at Waverly. The limited English of many parents made them reluctant to approach teachers with their questions and concerns. Without the active involvement and support of these parents, the challenge of providing their children with a sound education would be even greater.

Before a principal can address a challenge like the threat of school decline, he or she has to diagnose the school-based conditions that may need to be changed. The potential for incorrect diagnoses, of course, is ever present. There is no substitute for good listening skills, sound judgment, willingness to question standard operating procedures, and a commitment to doing whatever is necessary to serve the interests of children. Eli Buck possessed all of these attributes, and they helped him determine the leadership focus needed to address an increasingly diverse student body.

School decline, of course, may result from other impetuses besides changing demographics. In the following sections, three other decline scenarios will be discussed.

THE IMPACT OF INADEQUATE FUNDING

Economic conditions are roller coasters for public institutions like schools. When the local, state, or national economy sneezes, schools catch cold. The relationship between school funding and student achievement is well established (Darling-Hammond, 1997; Flanagan & Grissmer, 2005). In *Savage Inequalities,* Kozol (1991) provides disturbingly vivid examples of how funding disparities place students in poor school systems at a decided disadvantage. Even students in relatively well-off school systems may face the prospect of academic adversity when there is a downturn in the economy or a substantial loss of school funding. Such was the case in San Jose, California, following the passage of Proposition 13 in 1978 (Duke & Meckel, 1980).

Proposition 13 restricted the ability of localities in California to raise revenues by increasing property taxes. Since a substantial portion of school funding came from local property taxes, the impact was immediate and far-reaching. Stanford University researchers reported on how two consecutive years of 10 percent budget cuts affected one high school in San Jose (Duke & Meckel, 1980). It should be noted that the principal did not control all of the ways that the budget cuts were made. Some of the retrenchment decisions were governed by district policies and the teachers' contract. The principal, however, was expected to minimize the impact of *all* budget cuts on teaching and learning.

In 1979, the first year that Proposition 13–related cuts were implemented, San Jose High School enrolled 1,400 students, 65 percent of whom was Hispanic. Another 15 percent consisted of African American, Portuguese, and recently arrived Vietnamese students. Many students qualified for free and reduced-price lunch. Despite the principal's pleas that San Jose High School should not be cut as much as high schools in more affluent parts of the district, the central office insisted that all school budgets would be reduced by the same percentage.

To absorb the first round of cuts, San Jose High School released 14 teachers. They were collectively responsible for 44 classes. So great was the loss of classes, in fact, that the principal had to switch the schedule from a six-period to a five-period school day. This move had the immediate effect of limiting the course options available to students, eliminating teachers' planning periods, and increasing class sizes. The teacher-student ratio jumped to 1:31. More than 20 paraprofessionals also had to be released. Many of them came from the local community and spoke Spanish. Their departure meant the loss of a vital link between the school and non-English-speaking parents. The district even pressed the principal to eliminate the entire counseling department, but he was able to retain five counselors on the condition that each would teach several classes.

To accommodate the loss of faculty, six sections of English as a Second Language were dropped. An innovative reading remediation program was scaled back, and electives in music and industrial arts were eliminated. In most of these cases, the principal had little choice. Courses required for graduation could not be dropped. Seniority rules in the teachers' contract sometimes resulted in fully qualified teachers being "bumped" by less qualified but more senior teachers from other schools in the district. Eleven veteran teachers were transferred to San Jose High School in the fall of 1979. Under normal conditions, transfer teachers with limited experience teaching certain courses would be assisted by department chairs. Department chairs, unfortunately, also had been eliminated as part of retrenchment.

No area of school operations was spared. Extracurricular activities took an especially big hit. The band was disbanded, and approximately half of the sports program was cut. Physical education offerings also were curtailed.

Even the most capable principal may be unable to protect students and teachers from all the adversities associated with the kind of drastic cuts faced by San Jose High School. What principals must do to minimize the negative impact of such cuts is to anticipate where and how the reductions will be felt. This is an important aspect of organizational diagnostics—anticipating problems *before* they arise so that people can be forewarned and strategies for addressing problems can be developed. When parents, students, and school personnel are caught by surprise, the likelihood of serious school decline is greatly increased.

Given the cuts at San Jose High School, the principal understood the predictable fallout. Larger class sizes, the loss of special programs, and cutbacks in the time counselors had to counsel meant students were likely to receive less individual attention. Cuts to electives and extracurricular activities eliminated some of the school experiences most valued by students. Loss of ESL sections hit Hispanic and Vietnamese students especially hard.

The faculty of San Jose High School doubtless felt overworked and frustrated. With larger classes and no planning periods, the workload for teachers increased substantially. Discipline problems rose because students could not get the help they needed. Teachers were apt to adopt an informal triage system whereby students with the least chance of succeeding academically were all but abandoned. These students became prime candidates for dropping out. The combined effect of these circumstances led some of San Jose High School's most capable teachers to seek employment elsewhere. Attracting capable teachers to replace them was difficult.

As hopeless as the situation following substantial budget cuts might appear, many schools manage to avert a sustained downward slide. If they do, credit must go, in part, to an able principal who refuses to be caught off guard, who raises awareness of what can happen, and who sees to it that steps are taken to minimize the impact of budget cuts on teaching and learning.

THE IMPACT OF A WEAK PRINCIPAL

If capable leadership can be an antidote to school decline, the absence of capable leadership can serve as an impetus to school decline. Such was the case at Bluemont Elementary School in rural central Virginia.* When Sara Scott was chosen as Bluemont's new principal in the summer of 2004, she only had a few weeks to diagnose the damages that had resulted from her predecessor's lack of leadership. Scott was hired in July, and her teachers were scheduled to arrive in mid-August.

Bluemont enrolled 352 students, 88 percent of whom were white, and 9 percent of whom were African American. Approximately one-third of the students qualified for free and reduced-price lunch. Scott was relieved to discover that Bluemont's students tended to spend all six years of their elementary experience at the school. Of concern, however, was the fact that 18 percent of the students received special education services. The relatively high percentage alerted Scott to the fact that teachers may have been too quick to refer students to special education.

When Scott reviewed student performance on the state's third- and fifth-grade standardized tests in reading and mathematics, she detected the beginning of a downward trend. In the three years her predecessor had been at Bluemont, the passing rates for fifth graders had not improved, and the passing rates for third graders had declined.

The next step in Scott's diagnosis entailed a review of her faculty. She immediately noticed the high percentage of first- and second-year teachers, especially in the third grade. She also discovered that several teachers lacked the appropriate credentials in special education. What she did not find out until teachers returned to Bluemont for orientation was that the faculty was deeply divided. Apparently, Scott's predecessor had favored certain teachers over other teachers. The resulting resentment posed a challenge to Scott's plans to cultivate a schoolwide spirit of teamwork at Bluemont.

When the teachers arrived at summer's end, Scott learned more about why Bluemont was teetering on the brink of decline. Her predecessor had failed to share the results of state testing with the faculty. Teachers had no idea how their students had performed or what areas of reading and mathematics required attention. The previous principal also tended to deal individually with teachers. As a consequence, teachers worked alone rather than in teams. Bluemont lacked a school leadership team or grade-level teams. Apparently, Scott's predecessor was reluctant to share decision making with her faculty or nurture teacher leadership.

Knowing that many of Bluemont's students required additional help, Scott asked teachers about the kinds of assistance they provided for low achievers. She discovered that no programs of systematic and continuing assistance were in operation. If students did receive out-of-class aid, it was arranged on an individual basis with their teachers. Judging by Bluemont's test scores, whatever remedial instruction students received was not very effective.

---

*The author is indebted to Catherine Thomas for much of the information on Bluemont Elementary School. Bluemont Elementary School and Sara Scott are pseudonyms.

When Scott inquired about inservice training, she found out that there had been no school-based professional development during the preceding three years. To their credit, however, faculty members seemed receptive to learning more about strategies for raising student achievement. Scott hoped to capitalize on this interest by instructing teachers in how to make sense of their students' test results and provide targeted and timely assistance.

A veteran principal, Scott realized that immediate action would be needed if Bluemont was to be spared a period of sustained decline. Three years of ineffectual leadership had left the faculty adrift, divided, and unfocused and the community wondering what had become of their school.

THE IMPACT OF A CHANGE IN SCHOOL CULTURE

Educators who have spent time in different schools understand that schools can develop very distinctive organizational cultures. A school's culture encompasses professional and organizational values, beliefs about teaching and learning, and norms governing behavior (Sarason, 1982). Schools may be characterized by robust cultures, weak cultures, or the absence of a dominant culture. In the last instance, the school may consist instead of various subcultures. A robust school culture, of course, may not always constitute a positive force in the life of the school. In *The World We Created at Hamilton High,* Grant (1988) describes how a high school's culture changed for the worse. With the change came the threat of sustained school decline.

Located in an industrial city in the northeastern United States, Hamilton High (a pseudonym) started out as an elite public high school when it opened in 1953. Things began to change in 1966, however, when the school system began to implement a desegregation plan. At the time, only 90 African American students were enrolled at Hamilton High, but that number soon rose. By 1970, 210 African American students attended the high school. Racial tensions increased, and some white parents withdrew their children, but these developments alone do not explain why Hamilton High teetered on the edge of decline. Grant attributes much of the high school's troubles to bad judgments by the principal and the evolution of a school culture characterized by permissiveness and the abandonment of adult authority. The forces conspiring to undermine Hamilton High's reputation for academic excellence constituted a "perfect storm" that included a faculty's unwillingness to adjust to changing demographics, a principal's lack of leadership, and the development of a dysfunctional school culture.

According to Grant (1988), 1970 to 1971 was a pivotal year at Hamilton High. White teachers who had perceived black students to be industrious and well behaved when their numbers were small began to change their attitudes as the numbers of black students climbed. Teachers insisted that many of the new students were incapable of functioning in higher-level classes. As a result, basic classes consisted of large percentages of black students. To make matters worse, many white teachers disliked having to teach basic classes. Racial tensions led to violent incidents, and teachers and administrators spent an increasing amount of their time handling discipline problems. In the face of deteriorating conditions, veteran white teachers began to leave in droves. By the fall of 1971, 72 percent of the teachers who had taught at Hamilton High in 1966 had resigned, retired, or transferred. Personnel turnover, thus, can be added to the list of precipitants of school decline.

The principal correctly determined that drastic measures were needed to prevent the further escalation of problems. Rather than deciding to address school discipline and safety issues, however, he mistakenly concluded that Hamilton High's problems derived from its academic program. When the new school year began in the late summer of 1972, teachers were surprised to discover that the principal had unilaterally decided to eliminate all basic classes. Yearlong courses were replaced with semester and quarter-semester courses, and electives judged to be of greater relevance to students were introduced in place of many traditional academic offerings.

Replacing the departed veteran teachers were an assortment of young teachers whose sympathies clearly resided with their students. When it came to discipline, these teachers could best be described as lenient. They were slow to condemn students for drug use and inappropriate language, and they were less insistent on academic rigor than their predecessors. The school culture that began to emerge placed relatively little value on adult authority and academic excellence. Importance was placed on being able to address the varied needs of Hamilton High's students. The high school came to resemble more of a "social service center" than an academic institution. A variety of specialists offered programs on drug awareness, sex education, suicide prevention, and medical advice for pregnant teenagers.

Good intentions clearly were not enough to prevent Hamilton High from entering a period of sustained decline. By the time a new principal was chosen in the fall of 1977, enrollment had dropped by almost 300 students, absenteeism and behavior problems had reached alarming levels, and academic performance had plummeted. Teacher morale was low, and parent complaints were numerous. That Hamilton High eventually was put back on track is testimony to the impact of effective leadership. The leadership needed to turn around a troubled school like Hamilton High will be taken up in Chapters 3 and 4.

MEETING THE CHALLENGE OF SCHOOL DECLINE

One of the greatest challenges of school decline is recognizing the signs of decline early enough to address them effectively and avoid descent into an accelerating downward spiral. In his massive study of the collapse of entire societies, Jared Diamond (2005) identifies several precipitating failures. Failure to anticipate a threat and failure to recognize a threat once it has surfaced are two failures that can adversely affect organizations as well as societies (pp. 419–440). To meet the challenge of school decline, principals must understand the forces that can lead to decline and recognize the signs and symptoms of decline once they begin to appear. Chapter 1 has examined several potential sources of school decline, including demographic changes, sizable budget cuts, ineffectual leadership, and changes in school culture. These sources of decline may impact a school individually or in combination. Left unaddressed, they can lead to a variety of performance-undermining problems, including falling student enrollments, loss of community support, teacher turnover, and declining student achievement. Chapter 2 discusses some of the leadership actions a principal can take to prevent school decline.

KEY LESSONS AND NEXT STEPS

Eli Buck's first months at Waverly Elementary School offer several lessons to principals who confront a rapidly changing student body:

- A principal must be able to anticipate the needs of new students and assess the faculty's capacity to address these needs.
- Where capacity is lacking, provisions must be made for retraining the faculty.
- Potentially harmful practices such as pull-out programs and student retention at grade level should be reexamined.
- A principal must understand how parents feel about the school. This includes parents of new students as well as longtime residents.

Based on his assessment of the circumstances facing Waverly Elementary School and the potential for declining student achievement, what steps must Eli Buck take in order to prevent school decline?

Eli Buck must

- direct the faculty to focus on developing literacy in students with limited English proficiency,
- examine the school schedule in order to find additional time for English language instruction,
- identify effective practices and programs for English language learners, and
- consider how best to deploy Waverly's teachers in order to meet the needs of English language learners as well as other Waverly students.

2

Leadership to Prevent School Decline

The importance of focus was underscored in the Introduction. Faced with the kinds of complex challenges described in this book, school personnel must have a clear sense of direction and understand what the priorities are. Time, energy, and resources are rarely sufficient to allow educators to address everything that could be done to prevent a challenge from getting out of hand. It is the responsibility of principals to see to it that staff members know where to concentrate their efforts and why.

So what are principals who recognize the potential for school decline supposed to encourage their staffs to focus on? The answer depends to some extent on the source of potential school decline. In this chapter, one possible source of school decline will be addressed—changing demographics. When a school faces an influx of new students, especially if they are recent immigrants or come from impoverished homes, the focus must be on determining the educational needs of these students and assessing the school's capacity for addressing the needs. The remainder of this chapter explores in greater detail the leadership required to confront demographic change effectively.

LEADING SCHOOLS THAT
FACE DEMOGRAPHIC CHANGES

KEY QUESTIONS

1. What are the educational needs of new groups of students?

2. Does the school have the capacity to address these needs effectively?

3. If not, what actions must be taken to build school capacity?

4. What risks are involved in accommodating new groups of students, and how can the risks be minimized?

The Needs of Newcomers

The first order of business for principals who confront demographic changes involves determining the needs of newcomers. A half century ago, the newcomers typically were African American students who had gained access to previously segregated schools. Today, the newcomers often are foreign-born youngsters whose parents have come to the United States seeking economic opportunity and freedom from oppression, but they also may be children from poor families that move to previously homogeneous suburbs seeking a better life.

When Eli Buck studied the needs of his school's growing Hispanic population, there was no question about what his faculty's focus had to be. Waverly's newcomers needed to develop sufficient proficiency in the English language to benefit from instruction. Drawing on various assessment tools, Buck's reading specialist and English as a Second Language (ESL) teacher determined that Waverly enrolled 248 students at English Levels A and B in Grades K–5. Those were the lowest levels of language proficiency on a four-point scale. Almost 60 percent of the Title I students at Waverly were ESL students. Of the students who required development in phonemic awareness based on their Phonological Awareness Literacy Screening (PALS) test, 73 percent were ESL students.

After examining Waverly's capacity to address the needs of its newcomers, Buck concluded that most of his teachers were willing to do what they could to help Hispanic students, but they lacked the strategies and skills to do so. Professional development clearly would be required, especially with regard to teaching English to emergent readers. Buck believed that a significant portion of the needed inservice training could be provided by faculty specialists. He requested funds to hire another ESL teacher and a tutor to handle phonemic awareness. Two bilingual instructional assistants also were needed to assist teachers in the classroom as well as with school-home communications. Realizing that many of the newcomers required additional learning time in order to catch up to their peers, Buck asked for $57,000 to operate a monthlong summer program.

A school's capacity to address the needs of newcomers is not just about programs, professional development, and additional personnel. Beliefs and attitudes also must be considered. A few teachers at Waverly held low expectations for most Hispanic students. At the same time, they insisted that their approach to teaching was the correct one. Buck was unsure that any amount of professional development could overcome the resistance to change of these individuals. He prepared to confront the teachers, though the thought of doing so engendered considerable anxiety. Buck knew that these teachers were likely to point out that all of his experience had been at the secondary level. What did he know about the challenges of teaching young children? He did not pretend to be an expert on elementary education, but he refused to allow the hopes of so many children to fall victim to a few misguided teachers.

Buck decided on a two-pronged initiative involving summer school and changes in the assistance available to students during the regular school year. Summer school provided an opportunity for ESL students, especially the 21 who were recommended for retention in kindergarten and first grade, to receive additional time to develop language skills related to the state's learning standards.

Buck's plan for the regular school year centered on a variety of interventions, including a sheltered class for the first grade, the second grade, and the third grade. Sheltered classes are designed so that English language learners can receive grade-level instruction in the academic subjects using special materials and simplified English. Students address state curriculum standards while simultaneously developing their English language skills. This approach enables English language learners to keep up with their peers and eventually transition to regular classes. Each sheltered class is taught by a regular education teacher with the assistance of an ESL teacher and a reading specialist. Students leave their sheltered classes to attend electives, lunch, and recess with general education students.

For the fourth and fifth grades, Buck obtained the resources to operate a combined fourth-fifth-grade "newcomers" class. Meeting daily for a half-day, this class was led by a Title I and an ESL teacher. A mathematics resource teacher also provided instructional support.

Students who managed to progress in their language skills at a fairly rapid rate were assigned to inclusive classrooms in Grades 2, 3, 4, and 5. Bilingual instructional assistants were earmarked for the sheltered classes, though they could also be enlisted to provide assistance elsewhere. Reading Recovery, an intensive intervention for emergent readers, would be used at the first-grade level. The last piece of the puzzle involved the creation of a new school schedule that provided larger blocks of time for reading and language instruction as well as 45 minutes of extended learning time each day for reinforcement and remediation (see Figure 2.1). In

Figure 2.1   Waverly Elementary School Schedule

Times	K	1st	2nd	3rd	4th
8:15 – 8:30					
8:30 – 8:45	R	R	M	M	M
8:45 – 9:00	E	E	A	A	A
9:00 – 9:15	A	A	T	T	T
9:15 – 9:30	D	D	H	H	H
9:30 – 9:45	I	I	Specials		
9:45 – 10:00	N	N		R	R
10:00 – 10:15	G	G		E	E
10:15 – 10:30	Specials	M	R	A	A
10:30 – 10:45		A	E	D	D
10:45 – 11:00		T	A	I	I
11:00 – 11:15	Lunch/Recess	H	D	N	N
11:15 – 11:30		Lunch/Recess	I	G	G
11:30 – 11:45			N	Lunch/Recess	Specials
11:45 – 12:00			G		
12:00 – 12:15	M		Lunch/Recess		Lunch/Recess
12:15 – 12:30	A	E		E	
12:30 – 12:45	T	L		L	
12:45 – 1:00	H	T		T	
1:00 – 1:15	SS/Science	Specials	E	SS/Science	SS/Science
1:15 – 1:30			L		
1:30 – 1:45			T		
1:45 – 2:00	E	SS/Science	SS/Science	Specials	E
2:00 – 2:15	L				L
2:15 – 2:30	T				T
2:30 – 2:45	Math/Vocab	Math/Vocab	Math/Vocab	Math/Vocab	Math/Vocab
2:45 – 3:00	Enrichment	Enrichment	Enrichment	Enrichment	Enrichment

ELT = Extended Learning Time

order to explain Waverly's reforms to parents and enlist their support, Buck initiated an outreach program.

Preventing school decline is not a risk-free process. Buck understood that parents of students who were not newcomers might worry about how the various changes would affect their children. Despite his efforts to reassure these parents, some eventually chose to withdraw their children from Waverly. Other parents recognized, however, that the creation of sheltered and "newcomers" classes for the most needy ESL students would reduce the pressure on regular classroom teachers and enable them to address better the needs of general education students.

Buck lacked the funds to add classroom teachers, so he had to reassign certain faculty members to the newly created sheltered classes. While some Waverly veterans were willing to take on this challenge, others were not. The continued resistance to change of a small group of teachers interfered with Buck's efforts to build a schoolwide commitment to diversity and to ensure that all students succeeded. When Buck eventually moved on to a new principalship, however, he left knowing that Waverly was a better place for newcomers than it had been. Student achievement had not been allowed to decline, and programs to assist non-English-speaking and limited-English-speaking students were solidly in place. Hispanic parents expressed their gratitude for Buck's efforts to help their children.

Buck's success can be attributed to his focused leadership and unwillingness to ignore an emerging challenge. He saw to it that the educational needs of newcomers were carefully assessed. He evaluated Waverly's capacity to address these needs, and where capacity was lacking, he requested and obtained the resources needed to correct the situation. Buck understood that his efforts might not please everyone, but this realization did not deter him. Sometimes leaders must have the courage to do the right thing despite the likely consequences.

THE CHALLENGES OF CHANGING DEMOGRAPHICS

Several predictable challenges of changing demographics were discussed in the case involving Eli Buck's efforts to prevent academic decline at Waverly Elementary. There are, of course, many other challenges associated with an influx of students with backgrounds that differ from the traditional student population. Some of these additional challenges will be addressed in this section. They include variations among newcomer groups, nonacademic needs, choosing the most effective instructional approaches for newcomers, and confronting dysfunctional beliefs and attitudes regarding newcomers.

Variations Among Racial and Ethnic Groups

The metaphors vary from "melting pot" to "salad bowl," but no matter how people think about the makeup of American society, there is no disputing the fact that the United States is a highly diverse nation that is becoming increasingly diverse with each passing year. Public schools represent one of the primary stages on which the drama of diversity is played out. Consider the case of Fairfax County Public Schools in northern Virginia. In the 1960s when Fairfax desegregated, discussions of educational equity focused primarily on the school system's black minority. Fast forward to the 1990s and Fairfax County, by then host to the nation's twelfth largest school system, welcomed 112,841 immigrants (Duke, 2005, p. 70). The 2000 Census indicated that 237,677 of the county's approximately one million residents were foreign born. They included significant numbers of non-English-language groups, including speakers of Spanish, Vietnamese, Korean, Urdu, Arabic, Farsi, Chinese, Punjabi, Hindi, and Somali. Fairfax County Public Schools was expected to provide for the educational needs of each and every group.

Besides accommodating the vast number of foreign-born students as well as its longtime African American population, Fairfax also was faced with a growing number of disadvantaged students. Concealed by the fact that Fairfax County was one of the wealthiest counties in the United States, the burgeoning number of suburban poor generated challenges typically associated with urban school systems. By the spring of 2003, 23 percent of Fairfax's school-age population qualified for free or reduced-price lunch, and over 2,000 residents were estimated to be homeless (Duke, 2005, p. 72). Poverty's close companion is mobility. Principals in Fairfax schools grew accustomed to large numbers of students transferring in and out of school each year. The figure sometimes exceeded 40 percent!

It is tempting to use the phrase "changing demographics" as a catchall term representing recent immigrants, traditional American minority groups (African Americans, Native Americans), migrant workers, and the economically disadvantaged. This kind of general terminology obscures the substantial differences in cultural-historical backgrounds, status, and educational needs that can characterize each racial, ethnic, and socioeconomic group. Researchers investigating cultural discontinuity among the major minority groups in the United States are beginning to pinpoint some of the differences in values between mainstream American culture and the cultures of African Americans, Asian Americans, Latinos, and Native Americans. One study contrasted the mainstream American values of individualism and competition with an emphasis on communalism by African Americans, collectivism by Latinos, and cooperation and harmony with nature by Native Americans (Tyler et al., 2008). Assuming that many minority students do not shed their values at the schoolhouse door, school leaders need to be sensitive to situations where clashes in values may arise.

As if between-group differences were not challenging enough, there is reason to expect within-group differences as well. Research in the relatively new field of immigration studies, for example, is confirming the fact that some newcomers continue to identify with the culture of their former homelands while other newcomers embrace the popular culture of their new homeland or attempt to blend elements of both cultures (Arias, Faltis, & Cohen, 2007, pp. 108–112). These differences may influence how quickly and successfully newcomers transition to schools in their adopted country. The message for school leaders is clear—exercise care when generalizing about different groups of students.

Scholars long have been aware that some groups assimilate more readily into American society and attain higher levels of academic achievement than other groups (Ogbu, 2003). The reasons for these differences are the subject of considerable debate. While racial and ethnic bias, discrimination, and related structural factors obviously play a role, so too do forces within each minority group. Ogbu (2003) labeled these "community forces" and characterized some of them as "the ways minorities interpret and respond to schooling" (p. vii). When he investigated the black-white achievement gap in affluent Shaker Heights, Ohio, he discovered that the gap was a product not only of school policies and practices, including ineffective instruction and low teacher expectations for black students, but also of peer pressure not to excel in school or use Standard English, lack of parental guidance regarding how to negotiate the challenges of school, and greater interest by black students in conspicuous consumption than academic success.

Many scholars accept the fact that student achievement is closely tied to socioeconomic status. It turns out that family background and economic circumstances are greater determinants of student academic achievement for middle-class students than are school-based practices, programs, and policies (Frankenberg, 2007, pp. 14–15). Schooling, on the other hand, is more likely to have an impact on the achievement of students from disadvantaged backgrounds (ibid.). So why in affluent Shaker Heights did the children of highly educated and successful black parents still perform at lower levels than their white counterparts?

An equally perplexing question concerns the gap in achievement between Hispanic students and students from other non-English-speaking groups, such as Vietnamese, Chinese, Japanese, and Koreans. Once again, it appears that no simple explanation will suffice. Is there a cultural premium placed on education by the higher-achieving groups? Is socioeconomic status also a factor? When middle-class Cubans immigrated to the United States, they fared better in school than many less advantaged Spanish-speaking groups. Language differences alone cannot account for the achievement gap.

Assuming it is unwise and unwarranted to generalize about the needs of students from different racial, ethnic, and socioeconomic groups, imagine the challenge that faces educators in a highly diverse school. Differences among student groups must be understood and in most cases, valued without undermining the sense of cohesion and common mission on which public education depends. Different needs must be identified and addressed without appearing to be stereotyping or discriminating. Variations in backgrounds must be recognized without allowing such awareness to become a self-fulfilling prophecy (Weinstein, 2002).

Nonacademic Needs

Public schools are charged with meeting the academic needs of the students they serve. In order to do so, however, it may be necessary to consider a host of nonacademic needs as well. Human beings, for example, have a deep-seated need for affiliation and social support. This need can drive a teenage immigrant who feels alienated from the adolescent social milieu of his high school to seek affirmation and support from a gang. School leaders who understand this universal need for affiliation see that efforts are made to engage newcomers in team-based athletics and extracurricular activities such as chorus and theater that require group cooperation. They also work with community partners to develop youth organizations designed to engage young people in constructive projects when they are not in school. In *Urban Sanctuaries,* McLaughlin, Irby, and Langman (1994) describe the remarkable success of a variety of inner-city youth organizations, ranging from a Girl Scout troop to a gymnastics club. These groups provided sources of affiliation and support, but they also gave young people opportunities to exercise leadership, participate in the design of programs, and exercise control over their circumstances. When teenagers undertook activities in their "urban sanctuaries," the young people, many of whom had troubled backgrounds, no longer were put in the position of being "problems" to be "dealt with" (McLaughlin, Irby, & Langman, 1994, p. xi).

If affiliation and support function as the engines of healthy youth development, hope serves as the source of energy. Hope powers ambition. Without ambition, the road to academic success can turn out to be a dead end. When Ogbu (2003, pp. 252–253) investigated the achievement gap between black and white students in Shaker Heights, he found that students and their parents were conflicted regarding matters related to hope and ambition. Students and their parents expressed a desire to achieve success in adult life, but they questioned whether education would lead to success and acknowledged the impact of discrimination on the aspirations of blacks in the United States.

Researchers studying adolescent motivation have noted the tendency of some young people from disadvantaged backgrounds to have "misaligned ambitions" (Schneider & Stevenson, 1999, pp. 91–96). Consider the case of Rosa Lopez, who emigrated from Mexico with her mother when she was five years old. In California, Rosa's mother worked long hours at menial jobs in order for Rosa to have a shot at a better life. As a result of her work, Rosa's mother developed chronic back problems and complained of being in pain much of the time. Rosa was determined to become a physician and provide a better life for her mother. School was important to Rosa, but she failed to grasp what she needed to do in order to pursue a medical career. She missed a lot of school and often did not complete her homework. Challenging courses were dropped in favor of courses that were easier and more enjoyable. Rosa continued to cling to the dream of becoming a physician, but the decisions she was making in high school ensured that the dream would never become a reality. Her ambitions were not aligned with her actions.

School leaders can help students like Rosa by seeing to it that teachers and guidance counselors intervene early and provide a clear idea of what is needed to achieve ambitions. When students are uncertain about the careers available to them, they should be provided with timely information. Advice must not be offered in ways that discourage students, however. Keeping students informed about the steps required to attain challenging academic and career goals always should be accompanied by assurance of support and assistance when necessary. Public schools are not places where students' ambitions should be discouraged and hopes dashed.

Recognizing that classroom evaluations and grading practices can undermine student confidence and commitment to learning, Stiggins (2007) calls on educators "to embrace a new vision of assessment that can tap the wellspring of confidence, motivation, and learning potential that resides within every student" (p. 43). He urges greater attention to the "emotional dynamics" that surround "losing streaks" and "winning streaks" in classrooms. Teachers are encouraged to balance "assessment of learning" with "assessment for learning," the latter being based on helping students understand what success looks like and providing them with the constructive feedback necessary to achieve it. Simple strategies such as exposing students to work samples and enlisting them in developing practice tests can reduce much of the stigma associated with conventional classroom evaluation.

An important source of support for students from disadvantaged backgrounds is constructive role models. Research has found that teachers, mentors, and other adults to whom students can relate serve as guides for how to achieve desirable targets (Ormrod, 1998, pp. 437–446). When students are never exposed to exemplary models, either living or symbolic, that share their race, ethnicity, socioeconomic status, disabling condition, and gender, they are less likely to undertake challenging goals. Across the nation a variety of volunteer groups and professional organizations provide positive role models for students. One such group is the Society of Hispanic Professional Engineers (SHPE). SHPE members operate summer camps at various universities in order to attract more Hispanic students to careers in the so-called STEM fields—science, technology, engineering, and mathematics (Cech, 2008). Comparable groups are dedicated to assisting females, African Americans, and other minority groups in learning about career opportunities. When such groups are not locally available, school leaders should take the initiative and mobilize members of the community to create them.

Affiliation, hopefulness, and role models all concern psychological needs. Many students from disadvantaged backgrounds also have a variety of more tangible needs. When these needs—including adequate shelter, nutrition, and clothing—are not met, the chances for school success are markedly reduced. Working with various social welfare agencies, school leaders can make certain that students' physical needs are not neglected. In several locations, including Phoenix and San Diego, schools for homeless children have been established in order to facilitate the delivery of health, mental health, and nutritional services as well as educational services. While some critics complain that schools need to limit their mission to academics, educators who work with newcomers, migrant students, and students from impoverished homes understand that schools often are in the best position to address students' nonacademic as well as academic needs.

Needs typically are not limited to students either. The parents of newcomers and poor students also have needs. Helping parents can be a key to improving their children's chances of success. When parents do not speak English, schools can offer instruction in English as well as interpreters to facilitate home-school communications until parents acquire sufficient English to communicate on their own. Schools can operate early childhood education programs to provide preschoolers with opportunities for a "head start" while enabling parents to find employment during the school day.

Comprehensive educational reform initiatives like James Comer's School Development Program call for parents to spend time volunteering in classrooms and participating in school governance so that they can feel more connected to their children's education (Comer, 2004). When efforts were made to prevent Baskin Elementary School in San Antonio, Texas, from slipping into a downward spiral, school leaders implemented the concept of a learning community in which parents joined teachers, students, administrators, and other community members in making Baskin a true community center (*Hope for Urban Education,* 1999, pp. 55–56). Expanded hours of operation during evenings and weekends allowed faculty members, parents, and students to learn and work together.

Effective Instruction for Newcomers

One of the most perplexing challenges for school leaders faced with an influx of newcomers, especially newcomers with little familiarity with English, concerns the choice of an appropriate instructional model. In the preceding case of Waverly Elementary, Eli Buck wound up implementing a variety of instructional arrangements, depending on students' level of language development. School leaders should understand, however, that the selection of instructional models is not always a purely professional decision. Groups representing non-English speakers as well as other special interests actively lobby for particular approaches, thereby generating the potential for conflict and controversy.

When immigrant groups arrived on American shores in the late 19th and early 20th centuries, they frequently encountered public schools where they were forbidden to speak their native languages. Learning English as rapidly as possible was regarded as the key to acceptance and opportunity. In the second half of the 20th century, beliefs shifted as the value of proficiency in more than one language and the importance of cultural identity began to be recognized. While foreign-born students today are less likely to be punished for speaking their native languages, educators and policymakers debate the merits of different approaches to language development.

Some experts advocate *immersion,* where students learn in English and teachers use relatively simple language to instruct students in various curriculum subjects. *Transitional bilingual education* is an alternative approach in which students receive some instruction in their native language as well as concentrated English-language instruction. *Developmental bilingual education* focuses on building students' proficiency in their native language as they learn English as a second language. *Two-way immersion* calls for English speakers to learn a foreign language alongside native speakers, thereby providing an integrated learning environment.

Critics of bilingual education argue that it results in non-English speakers taking longer to learn English. As a consequence, they may not acquire sufficient English quickly enough to achieve academic success in school. In the aftermath of California's Proposition 227, which limited foreign language instruction for non-English speakers to one year, test scores for Latino students rose dramatically (Barone, 2002). This success did not keep advocates of bilingual education from attacking the measure for devaluing the culture and heritage of the foreign born. They insisted that students who develop proficiency in their native language eventually are able to acquire adequate skill in English.

The debate over how best to teach non-English speakers and limited-English speakers has taken on a new sense of urgency in light of the No Child Left Behind (NCLB) Act. English language learners (ELLs) constitute a subgroup under NCLB, and as a result, ELLs, regardless of how long they have been in the United States, are expected to make adequate yearly progress on state tests. The message is clear—ELLs need to learn English as quickly as possible. Schools are allowed to make "reasonable accommodations," including administering state tests in students' native languages, but only for a limited period of time. School leaders acknowledge confusion, however, regarding the appropriate length of time for "reasonable accommodations" to apply as well as what exactly constitutes the range of acceptable accommodations (Wright, 2007).

Because of the highly politicized nature of instruction for newcomers, decisions frequently are made at the school district and state levels. This does not mean, however, that school leaders have no role to play when it comes to addressing the academic needs of ELLs. Hawley (2007) points out,

> Student learning in schools is shaped not only by what happens in particular classrooms but also by the overall experience that students have as they witness and engage in interactions with peers, teachers, school administrators, and staff throughout the school. (p. 48)

The education of ELLs, as well as other minorities, is more likely to be a constructive experience when instruction addresses intercultural awareness and understanding. Furthermore, policies and processes should be in place at all schools for handling instances of perceived inequity and discrimination (Hawley, 2007, p. 49). Additional measures include hiring staffs that reflect diversity, providing staff with ongoing professional development on topics associated with meeting the needs of all students, and promoting schoolwide activities that value cultural differences (Hawley, 2007, pp. 49–50). Arranging summer programs to accelerate English-language acquisition and pairing English speakers with limited-English speakers for purposes of tutoring and intercultural awareness have proven to be helpful for newcomers. Whatever is done to enhance the instruction of ELLs, school leaders must ensure that these students receive high-quality teaching comparable to that provided other students. Lowering expectations and watering down content only serves to limit opportunities for newcomers.

Confronting Dysfunctional Beliefs

One of the greatest challenges associated with preventing possible school decline involves confronting dysfunctional beliefs. The varying needs of newcomers can be assessed and appropriate instructional methods can be identified and evaluated, but addressing harmful assumptions and attitudes is less straightforward and potentially more threatening. Sometimes people are unaware of their deepest beliefs about individuals who are unlike them. In other cases, they are aware of their beliefs but unwilling to acknowledge them publicly. Changing behavior is hard enough, but changing beliefs, especially those that have existed for years, can be truly daunting. Successfully confronting dysfunctional beliefs requires school leaders to exercise proactive leadership. The first step, however, may require school leaders to examine their own beliefs about newcomers.

McLaughlin, Irby, and Langman (1994, pp. 209–213) identify several "myths" that can block efforts to help inner-city youth. These myths also apply to many recent immigrants. One myth is that once at-risk youth reach adolescence, it is too late to help them. Two other myths are that inner-city youth are lazy and that they resist any effort to provide structure and discipline to their lives. In each case, the researchers found compelling evidence to debunk the myth. Given caring adults and engaging activities, inner-city teenagers demonstrated a remarkable capacity for initiative and achievement.

Much has been written about the impact of modest expectations for newcomers, traditional minorities, and students from impoverished homes. Ogbu (2003, p. 124) found that even in a community with many affluent African American families, teachers were perceived to believe that black students could not perform as well academically as white students. Furthermore, teachers expected black students to behave differently—to be inattentive in class and irresponsible regarding homework completion. For their part, guidance counselors were seen to be reluctant to assign black students to honors-level and Advanced Placement courses (ibid., p. 114).

When Gardiner and Enomoto (2006) studied urban principals who manifested "multicultural leadership," they found that these individuals promoted new beliefs about diversity. All students, for example, deserved to be subject to high academic expectations. Teachers were discouraged from assuming that all newcomers suffered from "cultural deficiencies." The principals understood that newcomers needed to be socialized to the norms and mores of their new country without denigrating their backgrounds and native cultures.

All teachers in a school ideally will share responsibility for addressing the needs of newcomers. Such a belief in collective accountability is absent, however, in many schools. Regular education teachers often consider the needs of newcomers to be the responsibility of ELL teachers, reading specialists, and special education teachers. Until these beliefs are challenged and changed, the likelihood of effective responses to demographic changes is relatively small.

Even educators who manifest great compassion for newcomers and other students who may be at-risk of academic difficulties can exhibit dysfunctional beliefs. McKenzie and Scheurich (2004) refer to these dysfunctional beliefs as "equity traps," which they define as "patterns of thinking and behavior that trap the possibilities for creating equitable schools for children of color" (p. 603). One such equity trap is "racial erasure." Payne (2008) describes how this equity trap works:

> Arguing "I am color-blind" may in fact reinforce the racial status quo. You cannot change racial inequality if you pretend that race isn't there. Color blindness gives the person claiming it the advantage of not having to think about how negative outcomes are distributed. (p. 27)

Faced with changing demographics, school leaders must encourage open and honest discussions of beliefs about racial and cultural differences. Only by sharing beliefs can educators come to appreciate the limits of "color-blindness" and understand the subtle impact of beliefs on practice.

Another equity trap involves "paralogical beliefs"—beliefs that derive from faulty premises. McKenzie and Scheurich (2004, p. 624) interviewed white teachers who admitted to losing control in class, screaming at their minority students, and occasionally treating these students in disrespectful ways. The teachers went on to attribute such problematic behaviors to the conduct of their students. Rather than believing that they controlled their own actions, in other words, the teachers blamed students for causing them to react inappropriately.

SCHOOL LEADERSHIP IN THE FACE OF DEMOGRAPHIC CHANGE

In order to address the needs of new groups of students and prevent good schools from becoming failing schools, school leaders must anticipate and be able to address a variety of challenges. They must recognize that cultural norms and academic needs vary within and across groups of newcomers. They must be aware of nonacademic as well as academic needs and make efforts to accommodate them in constructive and supportive ways. School leaders must stay informed regarding various approaches to instructing newcomers and take steps to advocate for the most effective approaches, even in the face of political pressure. Finally, school leaders must have the courage to confront dysfunctional beliefs about newcomers, in themselves and in others.

KEY LESSONS AND NEXT STEPS

Among the lessons learned from Eli Buck's efforts to address the needs of Waverly's nontraditional students and prevent a decline in student achievement are the following:

- Meeting the needs of nontraditional students is the responsibility of all faculty members, not just specialists.
- Instructional interventions for nontraditional students must be adjusted in accordance with their level of language development.
- Providing a high quality education for nontraditional students depends on changing dysfunctional attitudes and beliefs.
- Ongoing professional development that targets strategies for language development is crucial.

In order to continue the progress made under Eli Buck's leadership, his successor should consider these next steps:

- Identify and address the nonacademic needs of nontraditional students and their parents.
- Promote school activities that value cross-cultural understanding.
- Recruit new staff members who can serve as positive role models for nontraditional students.
- Coordinate school programs with community organizations and agencies concerned with the welfare of nontraditional students.
- Evaluate interventions for nontraditional students to make sure they are effective.

PART II

The Challenge of
School Turnaround

According to the *National Assessment of Title I*, 12 percent of all U.S. public schools (11,648 schools) were identified for improvement under the No Child Left Behind Act in 2005–2006 (Stullich, Eisner, & McCrary, 2007, p. 59). Almost one-quarter of these schools (2,771) had a history of failing to meet state standards for four to six years. These chronically low-performing schools are in need of many things, and inspired leadership tops the list. In order to turn around a school that has been characterized by low student achievement for years, a principal's first challenge is to determine where to begin. This may not be easy given the variety of problems that typically are found in low-performing schools. Successful "turnaround leaders" understand that several "quick wins" right off the bat can generate the confidence needed to tackle more difficult problems.

$$3$$

Identifying the Characteristics of Low-Performing Schools

A SCHOOL IN NEED OF TURNING AROUND[*]

Wilma Williams, a former middle school teacher and experienced elementary school principal, was chosen to participate in a state-sponsored program designed to turn around chronically low-performing schools. Keswick Elementary School, the school to which she was assigned, was located in a working-class city in the mid-Atlantic region of the United States and enrolled 237 students in Grades K–5. Over two-thirds of Keswick's students qualified for free or reduced-price lunch. One look at the school's standardized test data told Williams what needed to be done. How to do it, however, was not so clear.

One of every two third graders at Keswick failed to earn a "proficient" score on the state reading test, and a quarter of the fifth graders missed the mark. Proficient rates for third- and fifth-grade mathematics were 68 percent and 66 percent, respectively. Pronounced gaps existed in the failure

---

[*]The author is indebted to Kim Yates for much of the information on which the Keswick Elementary School case was based. Keswick Elementary School is a pseudonym, as is the name of the principal, Wilma Williams.

43

rates of white students and African American students. Students with disabilities also had a substantial failure rate.

Williams believed that the key to student success is a school's faculty. If students are not achieving, the first place to look has to be their teachers. Most of Keswick's 20 teachers were fully qualified, and several possessed master's degrees. Lack of proper credentials was not the issue. Williams turned next to the reading program. She noticed that classroom reading practices varied considerably from one teacher to the next. Most teachers, however, claimed that they followed a Montessori-based approach to reading. Williams' predecessor had introduced Montessori methods four years earlier, and Keswick's teachers expressed their support for the decision. Montessori-based reading instruction relies heavily on student self-pacing. Students are not "pushed" to acquire reading skills until they are "ready." Williams sensed that Keswick's low achievers might require a more structured approach to reading and a clearer set of expectations.

As Williams interacted with faculty members and learned more about how Keswick operated, she discovered other factors that might be contributing to student achievement problems. No procedures were in place for teachers to meet and analyze student performance on formative reading tests. Tests were aligned to state curriculum guidelines and administered every nine weeks. By reviewing student performance on these tests, teachers were supposed to be able to pinpoint areas where individual students could use additional assistance. No such systematic analysis was occurring. Furthermore, teachers were unaware of how particular subgroups of students, such as African American students and students with disabilities, were performing on the formative tests.

Williams next investigated what was being done at Keswick to help struggling students. The primary sources of assistance for poor readers were reading specialists. Students were pulled out of regular classes so they could work with a specialist. Williams doubted that this arrangement was helping very much, given the significant number of students who were failing to achieve reading proficiency. She understood the limitations of pullout programs and the fact that students who left class to see a reading specialist lost track of what their classmates were doing.

Concerned about the high failure rate of Keswick's students with disabilities, Williams investigated the special education program. She doubted the competence of one special education teacher but believed that this concern alone did not account for Keswick's problems. The fact that most students on Individual Education Plans (IEPs) spent most of the day in special education classes bothered Williams. Interaction with peers in regular education classes, she felt, was a critical component of effective education for students with disabilities.

As Williams concluded her assessment of conditions at Keswick Elementary School, she was careful to note several factors that the school had going for it. Keswick was relatively small, making it easier to envision the development of a true professional learning community. The school had relatively few discipline problems; therefore, Williams could devote much of her time and energy to bolstering the instructional program. Of greatest importance, Williams saw that the Keswick faculty genuinely cared for their students. She had confidence that teachers would be willing to make the changes necessary to raise student achievement and turn the school around.

ANALYZING THE CAUSES OF LOW PERFORMANCE

During Wilma Williams' first weeks at Keswick Elementary, she tried to understand what conditions might be contributing to low student achievement, especially in reading. It is indicative of her leadership that she did not dwell on conditions that were beyond her control. Instinctively, Williams focused on things that she could influence.

Deborah Stone (1989) uses the term *causal story* to represent an explanation that is offered to account for a public problem. She maintains that whenever there is dissatisfaction with an outcome in the public arena, various causal stories are advanced to explain it. Considerable politicking and conflict can characterize the competition among causal stories and for good reason. Whoever succeeds in having their casual story accepted is in a strong position to have their prescription for overcoming the problem adopted.

Today, many causal stories are presented to account for low-performing schools. It is important for school leaders charged with turning around these schools to understand the range of explanations they are likely to hear. It is equally important that school leaders understand the difference between a causal condition that they can correct and one that they cannot. Wilma Williams possessed such an understanding, and it enabled her to avoid dwelling on conditions she was powerless to influence.

One condition that school leaders are unlikely to change is poverty. They can help teachers and other staff members understand the implications of poverty, and they can sensitize individuals to the impact of poverty on the lives of students, but there is little they can do to raise the standard of living for the families they serve.

Poverty long has been recognized as a contributor to low student achievement (Rothstein, 2004). Many, if not most, low-performing schools enroll substantial numbers of students who qualify for free and reduced-price meals, a primary indicator of family poverty. Poverty undermines stable home lives for students, forcing parents to work long hours and compelling children to take on a variety of nonacademic responsibilities. School-age children of poverty may need to take care of younger siblings and obtain jobs to help make ends meet. The conditions in which poor families live may not be conducive to studying and completing school assignments. The advantages available to well-to-do families, including computers and books, are often absent. Poor families may have to move frequently in order to find employment and affordable housing. Because many poor children often have to switch schools, they are denied the instructional continuity and long-term relationships with teachers that can enhance their chances of succeeding in school.

A second condition associated with low student achievement is inadequate parenting, and this condition obviously is related to poverty in many cases. When parents express low expectations for their children, fail to encourage children to do their best in school, and reinforce dysfunctional behavior, they increase the likelihood that children will experience problems in school. When Clark (1983) compared the home life of high-achieving and low-achieving high school seniors, he discovered dramatic differences. The parents of high achievers initiated frequent contacts with school staff, established rules and norms related to completing school work, and communicated high expectations concerning post-secondary schooling. The parents of low achievers, on the other hand, had limited contact with school staff, set few rules regarding school work, and expressed modest expectations for post-secondary schooling.

Inadequate parenting is not intentional. Parents sometimes do not understand the impact that their behavior and beliefs can have on their children. In other cases, the pressure of domestic instability, divorce, and employment interfere with their desire to help their children do well in school. Parents who lack fluency in English can be at a disadvantage when it comes to keeping in touch with teachers.

As children grow older, peers can be added to poverty and parenting as a source of school-related problems. In some low-performing schools, the adolescent peer group may not value doing well in school. Good students may be ridiculed and subjected to taunts. The desire of young people to "fit in" leads some to abandon academic success as a goal and adopt habits and attitudes that lead to school problems.

Educators in low-performing schools sometimes express opinions that suggest nothing can be done to overcome the effects of poverty, parenting, and peers. School leaders confronted with the challenge of turning around low-performing schools realize that their first obligation is not to focus on conditions they are unlikely to impact, but to concentrate on conditions contributing to low achievement that they are able to correct. These conditions for the most part are school based. School leaders who cannot or will not recognize the ways that schools contribute to low performance are unlikely to achieve dramatic school turnarounds. The causal stories of successful "turnaround specialists" invariably focus on how school conditions contribute to academic problems and how educators' actions can overcome them.

DIAGNOSING SCHOOL-BASED CAUSES

When it comes to turning around a low-performing school, there is no substitute for leaders with expertise in organizational diagnostics. These individuals have the knowledge, instincts, and experience to recognize dysfunctional policies, practices, processes, programs, and personnel. Principals who have been in charge of schools that have been low performing for a long time, however, may not be able to recognize some of the school-based conditions that need to be changed. Such conditions become invisible over time. Lack of effective leadership, for example, is one condition many veteran school leaders are likely to overlook. It is hardly surprising, though, that 24 percent of schools in restructuring under No Child Left Behind were reported to have replaced principals (Stullich, Eisner, & McCrary, 2007, p. 55).

What are likely to be the conditions that confront a newly appointed principal of a low-performing school? Conditions can be divided into primary conditions and secondary conditions. Primary conditions involve student learning and behavior. Secondary conditions are school-based conditions that are likely to influence student learning and behavior. By identifying secondary conditions and focusing on improving them, school leaders can enhance student learning, raise academic achievement, and effect school turnaround.

Primary Conditions

While every low-performing school is likely to have certain unique features, all low-performing schools have one feature in common. A significant number of students struggle with aspects of literacy (Duke, Tucker, Salmonowicz, & Levy, 2007; Stullich, Eisner, & McCrary, 2007). Literacy problems, of course, subsume a variety of distinct issues, from vocabulary, reading comprehension, and phonemic awareness to listening and writing. Literacy is the key that unlocks the door to all subjects.

It is not unusual for many low-performing schools to be characterized by inadequate achievement in mathematics as well as literacy. Mathematics achievement becomes increasingly important as students advance in school. Algebra, for example, often is regarded as a "gatekeeper" subject. Students who struggle with Algebra I are less likely to understand the coursework in higher mathematics that is required to attend college.

Academic achievement is a function of exposure to good instruction. Students who miss a lot of school are at risk of falling behind in their assignments. Student attendance consequently constitutes another primary condition. Low-performing schools often are characterized by absenteeism rates that are much higher than other schools. Absenteeism, in turn, may be a function, in part, of discipline problems. When students disobey school rules, they are subject to suspension. If the offenses are serious enough, expulsion may even be warranted. Other students miss school not because they misbehave but because they fear for their own safety in school.

When a school is subject to high levels of absenteeism and behavior problems, teachers and administrators must devote a significant portion of their time and energy to checking on attendance and discipline. As a result, they are less able to concentrate on teaching and instructional support. A school facing such problems is doubly disadvantaged.

Secondary Conditions

If every school serving students from poor homes were characterized by problems with literacy, mathematics, absenteeism, and misconduct, school leaders might conclude that the negative impact of poverty was insurmountable. Evidence abounds, however, of high-performing, high-poverty schools (Chenoweth, 2007; Dana Center, 2002; *Hope for Urban Education,* 1999; Picucci, Brownson, Kahlert, & Sobel, 2002). That high-poverty schools can succeed suggests that chronically low-performing schools with large numbers of poor students must be contributing in some way to their academic problems. The first order of business for school leaders in these schools, therefore, is to determine what school-based conditions need to be improved.

In a survey of 430 schools identified as needing improvement under the provisions of the No Child Left Behind Act, school leaders reported requiring the following kinds of technical assistance in order to raise student achievement (Stullich, Eisner, & McCrary, 2007, p. 52).

Form of Assistance Reported to Be Needed	Percentage of Schools That Requested Assistance ($N = 430$)
Improve quality of teachers' professional development	80%
Get parents more engaged in their child's education	74%
Address instructional needs of students with IEPs	71%
Identify effective curricula, instructional strategies, or school reform models	70%
Improve students' test taking skills	70%
Analyze assessment results to understand students' strengths and weaknesses	68%
Identify or develop detailed curriculum guides, frameworks, pacing sequences, and/or model lessons aligned with state standards	62%
Develop or revise school improvement plan	62%

Form of Assistance Reported to Be Needed	Percentage of Schools That Requested Assistance ($N = 430$)
Recruit, retain, or assign teachers in order to staff all classes with a teacher who is "highly qualified"	62%
Address problems of student truancy, tardiness, discipline, and dropouts	57%
Implement the provisions of NCLB related to "qualified" paraprofessionals	52%
Address instructional needs of LEP students	49%

The greatest need for assistance concerned the professional development of teachers. Eighty percent of the responding principals indicated that the quality of professional development had to improve if their schools were to raise student achievement. Topics that might need to be addressed by professional development are suggested by other items, such as how to address the instructional needs of special education students (71%), how to improve students' test-taking skills (70%), how to analyze assessment results in order to understand students' strengths and weaknesses (68%), how to address truancy, tardiness, discipline, and dropout problems (57%), and how to address the instructional needs of students with limited English proficiency (49%).

Other areas in which assistance was perceived to be needed concerned responsibilities typically shouldered by school leaders. These included identifying effective curricula, instructional strategies, and school-reform models (70%), identifying or developing curriculum guides and related materials (62%), developing or revising school improvement plans (62%), and recruiting, retaining, and assigning teachers in order to staff all classes with highly qualified instructors (62%). Nearly three in four principals also indicated that they could use help in getting parents to be more engaged in their child's education.

These areas of needed assistance reflect many of the conditions that principals of low-performing schools actually target for change (Duke, 2006). They also correspond to problematic conditions identified by newly appointed turnaround specialists. When researchers (Duke, Tucker, Salmonowicz, & Levy, 2007) studied 19 first-year turnaround specialists, they found that the school-based conditions listed below were perceived to be associated with low levels of student achievement (the number of school turnaround specialists who identified each condition is in parentheses):

- Lack of focus (13)
- Unaligned curriculum (11)

- Ineffective instruction (16)
- Lack of data on student progress (15)
- Lack of teamwork (12)
- Lack of organizational infrastructure (10)
- Ineffective scheduling (9)
- Dysfunctional school culture (9)
- Ineffective instructional interventions (11)
- Lack of inclusion for special education students (8)
- Inadequate facilities (5)
- Inadequate instructional materials (3)
- Ineffective staff development (3)
- Personnel problems (18)
- Lack of specialists (5)

While no two turnaround specialists identified exactly the same set of problematic conditions, a number of conditions characterized many of the 19 schools. It is important to realize that these conditions represent aspects of school operations over which school leaders can exercise some degree of influence. The 19 turnaround specialists, in other words, did not attribute their schools' performance problems to factors beyond their control. Let us look more closely at each of the 15 secondary conditions.

Lack of focus. The importance of focusing energies on a limited set of organizational priorities already has been noted in this book. It is tempting, of course, for school leaders in low-performing schools to think that everything is a high priority. When everything is treated as a high priority, though, then nothing is a high priority. Accounts of low-performing schools frequently point out that staff members feel adrift. They lack a clear sense of direction. They complain of feeling as if they are running in all directions at once. Without a focused mission and limited set of specific improvement targets, it is difficult for school leaders to know how to allocate scarce resources and to determine if their efforts are producing desired results.

Unaligned curriculum. As a result of the No Child Left Behind Act and state educational accountability systems, students are expected to master various content-based objectives spelled out in state and local curriculum guidelines. To ensure that students learn this content, states have developed or adopted standardized tests based on the curriculum guidelines. One reason why some schools are designated as low performing is that students are not being taught content based on these state curriculum guidelines and aligned to the state tests. In some cases, little effort has been made to have teachers design lessons according to the approved content standards. In other cases, curriculum alignment efforts have been made, but school leaders have failed to monitor classroom instruction carefully. As a result, some teachers teach what they want to teach. Many students consequently struggle with the state tests because they have not been exposed to the required content.

Ineffective instruction. One of the conditions most frequently noted by the turnaround specialists was ineffective instruction. Ineffective instruction goes beyond failing to teach required content. It involves how well content, required or not, is taught. The turnaround specialists noted such concerns as failing to inform students of lesson objectives and giving students directions that were unclear or misleading. Teachers in these low-performing schools often neglected to differentiate instruction based on student needs and reteach material to students who did not get it right the first time. Lessons frequently lacked the high degree of structure that many at-risk students need. Considerable instructional time was lost because teachers had to deal with classroom management issues. Other instructional concerns included lack of careful planning and ineffective use of homework.

Lack of data. Another frequently mentioned condition involved the absence of regularly collected data on how well students were learning required content. Failure to employ good classroom assessment practices meant that teachers often were unaware that certain students were struggling. When teachers eventually tested students, considerable time had passed and some students had fallen far behind their classmates. Teachers did not regularly review student performance on tests in order to identify patterns of error and misunderstanding.

Teachers in many of the low-performing schools did not meet by grade-level or subject matter area to review student performance on state tests. Benchmark or formative tests aligned to state curriculum standards were not used in some schools as a means for regularly monitoring student progress. The lack of timely data on student progress handicapped efforts to provide students with targeted assistance.

Lack of teamwork. The failure of teachers in many low-performing schools to meet and review student test data was symptomatic of a more general lack of teamwork. Teachers tended to work in isolation. Academic and behavioral issues were rarely addressed collectively. Teachers did little planning in groups. When teachers did band together, they typically did so to defend themselves against criticism or resist recommended changes. The turnaround specialists' predecessors often found it difficult to mobilize their faculties for school improvement initiatives. Teachers seemed to have accepted low performance as inevitable.

Lack of infrastructure. To some extent, the lack of teamwork can be regarded as a function of the lack of organizational infrastructure in many of the low-performing schools. Grade-level teams, vertical teams devoted to articulation across grade levels, school improvement teams, and leadership teams frequently were missing. What was unclear to the turnaround specialists was whether the absence of organizational infrastructure was a cause or a consequence of lack of teamwork. Some of the low-performing schools were characterized by deep divisions among faculty members. It could have been the case that teacher groups had been abandoned because they served as opportunities for arguments and rancor. Whatever the reason, the lack of organizational arrangements for teachers to work together was perceived by principals to undermine academic improvement efforts.

Ineffective scheduling. It takes time during the school day for teams of teachers and school leaders to collaborate on analyzing student achievement data, developing lesson plans, and aligning the curriculum with state standards. Time also is needed to plan and implement interventions to help struggling students. Whether adequate time is available to support these activities is a function of the school schedule. Turnaround specialists frequently noted that low-performing schools lacked a daily schedule that facilitated teamwork and instructional interventions. In order to plan, teachers were forced to meet, when they met at all, after school. Student assistance, when available, tended to be delivered on an ad hoc basis during the school day.

Dysfunctional school culture. Schools, even low-performing ones, can be characterized by distinctive cultures. School cultures consist of shared beliefs about students, teaching, and learning. They also embody norms that govern how people relate to each other and how work is carried out. Some of the turnaround specialists commented on the negativity of their schools' cultures. Teachers expressed the belief that many of their students were incapable of mastering content. Instead of focusing on the continuous improvement of instruction, faculty members dwelled on making excuses for low performance and blaming conditions beyond their control. More emphasis tended to be placed on controlling student behavior than caring for students. Teachers who made suggestions regarding ways to improve teaching and learning sometimes were subjected to ridicule and ostracism in these dysfunctional cultures.

Ineffective interventions. Efforts were made in all 19 low-performing schools in the study to help at least some struggling students. The widespread lack of student success in these schools, however, led a number of the turnaround specialists to perceive that most efforts to help were ineffective. Sometimes the problem concerned who delivered the help. Volunteers and teachers who lacked training in instructional assistance were not equipped to provide effective help. In other cases, interventions were not targeted to specific problems. Instead, students simply were assigned to a program where they spent additional time doing a variety of things, many of which were unrelated to their particular learning issues.

Lack of inclusion. One of the student subgroups that contributed to the schools' low performance was special education students. The turnaround specialists noted in some cases that these students spent most of the day in self-contained classes rather than in regular classes. As a result, special education students were less likely to be exposed to the content upon which they eventually would be tested. In addition, they felt isolated from their peers and stigmatized.

Inadequate facilities. In a few cases, turnaround specialists expressed concerns about the quality of the facilities in which students were required to learn. Learning in rooms that are cramped, poorly lit, inadequately ventilated, and unattractive can be challenging for students and their teachers. When schools are unclean and poorly maintained, when paint is peeling and roofs leak, the message to those who study and teach in school is far from affirming. Neglected physical space bespeaks a general lack of concern on the part of those responsible for supporting public schools.

Inadequate materials. Several turnaround specialists noted that their schools lacked appropriate instructional materials. Textbooks either were in poor condition or lacking entirely. Maps were outdated. Computers were in need of repair. As in the case of run-down facilities, inadequate materials send a negative message to students and teachers in desperate need of help and hope.

Ineffective staff development. Efforts had been made in most of the low-performing schools to provide teachers with some form of staff development. In a few cases, though, this staff development was judged to be ineffective. Either it was too highly generalized to be of practical value or it was not linked to programs in place at the school. Another component of ineffective staff development involved the failure of outside resource people to work with teachers over an extended period of time. So-called one-shot workshops were regarded as relatively unproductive, given the extensive needs of teachers in chronically low-performing schools.

Personnel problems. All but one of the turnaround specialists identified personnel problems as one of the conditions that had to be addressed in order to turn around their schools. If teachers are key factors in student success, it is only logical that they also play a role in student failure. Turnaround specialists reported that some faculty members, especially those in special education, lacked appropriate credentials. In other cases, the problem concerned teachers who were resistant to change. Low-performing schools tend to have high turnover rates. As a result, many teachers are in their first or second year of teaching. These individuals often lack the experience and expertise to provide effective instruction for students performing well below grade level. The turnaround specialists complained that their predecessors had not always identified teachers' deficiencies or placed marginal teachers on plans of assistance.

How teachers see it. It is worth noting that teachers in low-performing schools may not necessarily identify the same problematic conditions as school leaders. In a survey of 7,394 elementary teachers, the challenges to improving student achievement that were identified included insufficient parent involvement (80%), low student motivation (75%), large class size (62%), too few textbooks and instructional materials (33%), and textbooks and instructional materials that are not aligned with state standards (18%; LeFloch et al., 2007, p. 91). It is revealing that the teacher respondents did not identify any challenges related to the competence of instructional personnel. If these teacher-identified conditions are indicative of the views of teachers in all low-performing schools, they point to yet another possible condition associated with low performance—the lack of agreement between teachers and school leaders regarding the causes of inadequate student achievement.

MEETING THE CHALLENGE OF SCHOOL TURNAROUND

Early detection was the key to preventing school decline in Chapter 2. School leaders who face the challenge of turning around a low-performing school are denied the opportunity for early detection. They face conditions that have been in place for some time. Some of these conditions, such as poverty and inadequate parenting, are beyond their control. Other conditions, however, are school based and therefore within the sphere of influence of school leaders. These conditions can be divided into primary and secondary conditions. Primary conditions pertain to student performance and conduct. Secondary conditions are associated with school personnel, policies, practices, processes, and programs. They include inadequate instruction, lack of teamwork, and ineffective scheduling.

After years of low performance, school personnel sometimes assume that little can be done to improve these conditions. Payne (2008) characterizes chronically low-performing schools as "demoralized environments" (p. 41). He goes on to note an insidious quality of such environments. Staff members actually can become invested in the failure of those around them. When others fail, these individuals no longer need to bear the burden of low performance alone. As Payne (2008) puts it, "Institutional failure can create a social environment that encourages yet more failure, one downward spiral generating another" (p. 45).

A low-performing school is unlikely to be turned around unless and until students believe they are capable of academic success. Students are unlikely to believe that they are capable of academic success unless and until their teachers believe in their own capabilities as teachers. What school leaders need to do to build the necessary confidence in their faculties is the focus of Chapter 4.

KEY LESSONS AND NEXT STEPS

Wilma Williams' initial efforts to understand what was needed to turn around Keswick Elementary School provide several lessons for principals faced with similar situations:

- It is important to distinguish between causal conditions over which principals can and cannot exercise some control.

- Practically all chronically low-performing schools share one thing in common—literacy problems.
- Not all literacy programs are equally effective.
- Students who struggle with literacy are likely to need highly structured instructional programs.

Following Wilma Williams' preliminary diagnosis of problematic conditions at Keswick Elementary School, what steps are likely to be needed in order to initiate the turnaround process?

- A clear set of priorities and targets for improvement are required in order to give the faculty a sense of direction.
- The existing reading program must be replaced with one that provides students with greater structure.
- Several "quick wins" must be achieved in order to demonstrate that the new principal can "get things done."
- Teachers must be encouraged to assume responsibility for raising student achievement.

4

Leadership to Turn Around a Low-Performing School

Principals who are expected to turn around low-performing schools need to establish a clear and coherent focus as much as principals faced with possible school decline. The nature of the focus and how it is addressed, however, are likely to differ in important ways from situations involving the prevention of school decline. Avoiding a drop in student achievement in a school that has performed reasonably well is one thing; reversing years of inadequate student achievement is quite another matter. Leading the school turnaround process requires a great deal of what, for lack of a better term, can be called persuasion. Staff members need to be convinced that they possess, or can acquire, the competence to provide high quality instruction. School district leaders must be persuaded that additional support during the turnaround process is a good investment of resources. Parents and community members must be sold on the idea that improvements can be achieved quickly, without sacrificing an entire cohort of young people. Last, but certainly not least, students must believe that their hard work and persistence will be worth it.

The ultimate success of all this convincing depends a lot on the ability of school leaders to act quickly, decisively, and judiciously. Principals who take the position that "it can't get any worse" and who grasp at any new initiative in an effort to raise achievement may be able to act quickly and decisively, but they are not exhibiting sound judgment. Conditions always can get worse. Students, even those in the lowest-performing schools, are not guinea pigs for whom any experiment is justified. It is essential that school leaders adopt only those strategies that are likely to make a positive difference.

TARGETING KEY CONDITIONS

KEY QUESTIONS

1. What should be the primary focus of school turnaround efforts in the first year of the process?

2. Can school leaders achieve a few "quick wins" in order to mobilize faculty and community support?

3. What can be done to raise teachers' confidence that they can achieve school turnaround?

4. What conditions may take somewhat longer to correct?

The Need for Direction

Principals who have been through the school turnaround process understand the value of establishing a clear sense of direction and gaining widespread commitment to it. The two greatest problems facing many chronically low-performing schools are drift and detachment. Professionals and patrons alike are unsure where these schools are headed, and few people are willing to make a wholehearted commitment to school improvement when the targets are vague. Having said this, it must be noted that achieving a clear and coherent focus is no simple, straightforward matter. So much needs to be done in most low-performing schools that the act of agreeing on where to begin and what to focus on constitutes a major challenge in and of itself.

It is likely that different people will hold different views regarding what "first steps" need to be taken. School principals, therefore, should be prepared to take the lead, in the absence of consensus, in establishing a credible focus for the first year of the school turnaround process. There are always trade-offs to be made when choosing a specific direction for improvement. A focus on reading may preclude, for the time being, a focus on math. When teachers and parents express varying opinions regarding the best focus for the first stages of school turnaround, prudence dictates that school leaders take the initiative to articulate a focus. Taking such action can prevent the polarization of the faculty and the community and allow turnaround efforts to get off the launching pad.

When Wilma Williams assumed the principalship of Keswick Elementary, she knew the school faced a variety of challenges, but she harbored no doubts about what the initial focus needed to be. Literacy! Reading scores were slipping. Williams understood that, as reading goes, so goes achievement in other subjects.

It should be noted that turnarounds at the secondary level may involve a somewhat broader focus. Reducing the retention rate, raising the percentage of students who graduate, and eliminating low-track classes are some of the key targets for middle and high school principals charged with turning around their schools. At the elementary level, however, improving student achievement in reading and other aspects of literacy is frequently the first focus of attention. This chapter will address the challenge of turning around low-performing elementary schools when literacy is the central concern.

To appreciate how Williams undertook her turnaround efforts, it is instructive to examine her key decisions over the course of her first year at Keswick. During the summer, she met with teachers, parents, and central office personnel and listened to their explanations for Keswick's low reading scores. She concluded that a primary cause involved the school's previous adoption of Montessori methods. As she put it,

> Primarily because of the Montessori approach, there was no defined reading or math program at the school. Each teacher had the freedom to develop their own program that moved students along at their own pace. Needless to say, some students were not moved along as far as others. This lack of progress was attributed to students' developmental differences and tolerated under the Montessori philosophy.

Based on her experience as an educator, Williams realized that students who were allowed to lag behind their peers often failed to catch up later. As long as the Montessori program remained in place, teachers would have a convenient excuse to account for some students' slow progress. As the new school year began, Williams announced that the Montessori program had to be abandoned. In its place, teachers were instructed to use the Scott Foresman reading program that had been purchased for the Keswick faculty several years before but never implemented. The Scott Foresman program provided the structure and sequencing of skills that had been missing in the Montessori approach. After obtaining the approval of the central office, Williams and her Title I coordinators met with Scott Foresman representatives to order updated materials and arrange for a staff developer to reintroduce the program to the Keswick faculty. It is telling that Williams never accepted the notion, held by some of her staff, that certain Keswick students were unlikely ever to be strong readers. If some students struggled with reading, it was the fault of the reading program, or more accurately, the lack of a reading program.

Before Williams' arrival, no set schedule for reading instruction existed at Keswick. The amount of time devoted to reading varied considerably from one teacher to the next. Williams decided that reading instruction would occur every day between 8:30 and 10:00 in the morning. In order to reduce the size of reading groups and increase the likelihood that every student received more attention, all professional staff members were enlisted to teach reading during the daily reading time. Even the librarian and physical education teacher conducted reading groups. By involving all faculty members in Keswick's reading program, Williams demonstrated what the primary focus of school turnaround efforts was going to be. Besides the 90-minute reading time every morning, 40 minutes at the end of every school day was set aside to provide help for students who had encountered difficulties during the day's reading lessons. Williams hoped that by staying on top of problems, students would not fall too far behind their classmates.

Williams realized that mandating a reading program and providing staff development were necessary but not sufficient to ensure improvements in student literacy. A system for monitoring student progress and holding teachers accountable was needed to accompany implementation. Keswick had a benchmark testing program aligned to the state's literacy standards, but it was not being used effectively. Instead of administering the tests every nine weeks, as her predecessor had done, Williams opted to test students every four-and-a-half weeks. That way, teachers would have a more frequent source of feedback on student progress and be able to provide assistance in a more timely and targeted manner. The school schedule was adjusted so that groups of teachers (K–1, 2–3, 4–5) could meet and review the results of the benchmark tests during the regular school day. Test results were disaggregated by student subgroup, according to federal guidelines, and students were placed in quartiles based on their performance. Assignment to reading groups and special interventions was based on the quartile in which each student was placed. Williams sat in on teacher meetings to ensure they were productive.

By December of her first year, Williams' assessment of the benchmark testing results led her to believe that a supplemental reading program was needed for Keswick's weakest readers. She secured support from the central office to purchase the Breakthrough to Literacy Program with Title I funds. Breakthrough to Literacy is a comprehensive program that includes big books, take-home books, and an individualized software instruction program that requires listening to the book-of-the-week, think time, vocabulary and comprehensive exercises, word puzzles, reading along with the book-of-the-week, explore words, alphabet, and spelling. Along with the program came additional staff development and computers for each classroom in Grades K–3. To further bolster efforts to help struggling readers, Williams sought and received permission from the superintendent to use her special education reading intervention specialists and Title I reading specialists in regular classes rather than only in pullout classes.

Finally, just before the administration of state tests in the spring, Williams initiated an afterschool reading and writing assistance program for students whose previous benchmark tests indicated deficits. What is noteworthy about Williams' approach to raising reading achievement was her reliance on a continuum of interventions. While the first line of defense against reading problems was structured and systematic instruction by regular classroom teachers, these efforts were backed up by a variety of sources of focused assistance. The delivery of focused assistance was dictated by regularly collected and reviewed data on student progress.

Turning around a low-performing school requires a bias for action, but it also demands good judgment. Evidence of Williams' good judgment can be found in her decision to postpone replacing the Scott Foresman reading program. By mid-year, she had determined that Keswick students would benefit from an even more highly structured reading program, one that actually scripted much of what teachers were to say and do with students. She began discussions with representatives of the SRA program but concluded that her faculty had undertaken enough change for the school year. She elected to wait until the summer to begin training teachers in the SRA program.

Two years were required for Wilma Williams and her faculty to turn around Keswick Elementary. By 2007–2008, Keswick made adequate yearly progress and was fully accredited by the state. The percentage of third graders passing the state test in reading was almost 90 percent. Substantial gains also were posted for other grade levels and subject areas.

Wilma Williams' efforts are indicative of what other elementary principals have done to turn around low-performing schools (Duke, Tucker, Salmonowicz, & Levy, 2008; Hope for Urban Education, 1999; Jacobson, Brooks, Giles, Johnson, & Ylimaki, 2004). Given the fact that low elementary school performance typically involves problems with literacy, establishing a focus on raising student achievement in reading and related subjects makes considerable sense. As is seen in the case of Wilma Williams, however, determining a clear direction is only the beginning of the journey to higher student achievement. In the next section some of the other steps that school leaders may need to take to ensure a successful turnaround will be reviewed.

Before addressing these "next steps," however, it is important to comment on the choice of a literacy program. Given the expense of researching and developing a literacy program, many schools and school systems rely on purchasing commercial programs. School leaders may not be reading specialists, but they need to know what questions to ask in order to assess whether a particular program is well suited to the needs of their schools. Wilma Williams initially determined that the Scott Foresman program was preferable to the Montessori approach favored by many of her teachers.

When student reading achievement was not improving as much as she felt it should, she explored other options.

Successful school turnarounds have involved a variety of literacy programs. Low-performing elementary schools in Richmond, Virginia, for example, benefitted from the Voyager Passport reading program. The Dodge Renaissance Academy, a K–8 school in Chicago, got impressive results following the adoption of a "balanced literacy" approach (New Leaders for New Schools, 2008, p. 32). Wilma Williams would have felt uncomfortable with this approach, given the fact that it rejects scripted exercises and basal readers. The point is that there is no "one best" literacy program, but some programs are a better fit for student needs and teacher strengths than others. Choosing an appropriate program is a matter of judgment. The more school leaders know about the elements of a sound literacy program, the more they will be able to ensure that an appropriate selection is made.

The Importance of "Quick Wins"

It goes without saying that school leaders cannot achieve a turnaround by themselves. Principals charged with turning around a low-performing school often are new to the school. To secure the support of teachers and community members, they must demonstrate their ability to get things done. The most challenging problems typically take more time to resolve, so school leaders need to identify a few concerns for which they can achieve some "quick wins."

Student behavior. One such issue involves classroom management and school discipline. An orderly learning environment is a prerequisite for raising student achievement. When teachers and administrators must spend precious time dealing with discipline problems, they are less able to focus on academic improvement. Parents grow concerned when they hear about misconduct and disruptive behavior in school.

The case of Jarvis Sanford, the new principal of the Dodge Renaissance Academy mentioned earlier, illustrates a "quick win" related to student behavior:

> He immediately spelled out clear expectations for student behavior, such as how students would walk in lines in hallways, and enforced these expectations consistently. He also made sure the staff modeled these expectations and established norms of respect; for example, he instituted a dress code for faculty and pitched in himself as a substitute teacher to show that everyone has a responsibility for maintaining the school culture. (New Leaders for New Schools, 2008, p. 11)

Spelling out clear expectations for student behavior and enforcing those expectations fairly and consistently are essential steps in creating orderly learning environments. They are not a substitute, however, for positive relationships between students and staff members. When students feel they are not respected and cared for by adults in the school, they come to regard disciplinary measures as punitive.

Another key to reducing behavior problems involves teaching students about school rules, why rules are important, and the consequences for breaking rules (Duke, 2002, pp. 66–68). In some schools, students actually must pass a test on the rules of conduct. For younger students, role-playing expectations for classroom behavior also can be helpful. To balance an emphasis on reducing negative behavior, teachers and administrators need to reinforce students when they behave appropriately. Encouraging good behavior generally has been found to be more effective than punishing bad behavior (Duke, 2002, pp. 76–77).

Some low-performing schools are located in neighborhoods that are considered to be dangerous. When students feel unsafe coming to and leaving school as well as while they are in school, they are less able to focus on learning. Principals charged with turning around a school can achieve an important "quick win" by working with local law enforcement officials, community members, and school district security personnel to ensure student safety. Measures may include recruiting adult volunteers to walk with young students to school and ensuring that all staff members understand the provisions in the school crisis management plan. A study of three school turnarounds in New York found that the principal in each case began by physically securing the building (Jacobson et al., 2004, p. 31). These efforts included limiting access to the building, screening visitors, and making certain that doors were locked.

Another aspect of student behavior where improvements can be achieved relatively fast is attendance. Many low-performing schools have relatively high rates of absenteeism and tardiness. School leaders can work with parents to initiate a campaign to reduce absenteeism. If some parents remain uncooperative, it may be necessary to engage the local juvenile court judge to ensure students are in school. When J. Harrison-Coleman confronted absenteeism and tardiness at Stephen H. Clarke Academy in Portsmouth, Virginia, she involved the police (Duke et al., 2005). Parents had been in the habit of coming to school in the afternoon and pulling their children out of class without obtaining the permission of the principal. With police assistance, parents began to cooperate and go to the office to sign out their children. The number of students leaving school early dropped dramatically. In order to reduce the high rate of absenteeism on Fridays, Harrison-Coleman launched "Dancing Into Friday." Students, parents, teachers, and staff members gathered in front of the school every Friday morning and danced to popular music before classes began. Friday absences immediately fell.

Faculty commitment. School leaders engaged in turning around low-performing schools generally inherit a faculty. Securing the support of a substantial number of faculty members is critical. Terms such as *trust, buy-in, ownership,* and *commitment* are often associated with the acquisition of faculty support. New principals frequently begin their efforts to enlist teachers in the turnaround process before school begins. They meet over the summer with teachers, either individually or as a group, to discuss the challenges ahead. Principals learn what teachers think about the sources of low performance and how they can help address the improvement of student achievement. Unless teachers feel that their voices are valued, they are unlikely to support a new leader.

Every school, no matter how low performing, has some positive aspects. One strength might be a cadre of dedicated teachers. Other strengths could include an award-winning club, a business or community partnership, or a parent volunteer program. New school leaders need to recognize these benefits if they are to enlist people in the school turn-around process. While considerable time in low-performing schools must be spent analyzing why some things are not working well, it is also important for school leaders to understand why certain aspects of the school are working reasonably well. Often, the knowledge gained in this way can be built on to promote additional successes. Staff members appreciate it when a new principal does not overlook "pockets of promise."

Teachers are unlikely to value a new principal's leadership unless they feel that the principal understands their students and the conditions in which they must teach. Spending time in classrooms is the best way to develop such understanding. Time in classrooms also provides opportunities for school leaders to model effective approaches to instruction and classroom management. In writing about Muriel Leonard's successful efforts to turn around Robert Gould Shaw Middle School in Boston, Leader (2008) notes,

> Leonard was not above modeling for her staff. If managing a class of unruly youths seemed impossible, Leonard took a shot at it herself. If she asked teachers to devote time to developing student products, she devoted the time as well. If the task was disaggregating quantitative data from tests or attitude surveys, Leonard was there pitching in. (p. 216)

In a study of new middle school principals' efforts to turn around a low-performing California school, Britz (2007) found that 83 percent of the teachers reported that the new principals established credibility within the first 90 days. Some of their explanations were revealing:

> In our first meeting, she listened to the concerns I had, wrote them down and did something to solve them.

> First week of school, she visited all classes and followed the visits with positive notes to the teachers.

I had a personal problem and shared it with her. Friday of that week, she covered my afternoon classes, and sent me home early. (pp. 104–105)

While there is no substitute for good relations with teachers, new principals also must be careful to keep relationships on a professional level. Becoming too friendly with staff members can make it difficult for school leaders to provide constructive feedback, evaluate teaching performance, and communicate high expectations.

Environmental improvements. Another target for "quick wins" is the school structure and its surroundings. The image of low performance frequently is reinforced by facilities and grounds that are poorly maintained. When J. Harrison-Coleman began her efforts to turn around Stephen H. Clarke Academy, she met with her custodial staff and impressed upon them the importance of keeping the hallways uncluttered. She also negotiated with the central office to get a fresh coat of paint for the interior of the school. Melva Belcher focused more on the external environment when she took the helm at Westside Elementary in Roanoke, Virginia. The school's deteriorating playground area had become a local hangout. She insisted that the broken glass be cleaned up and the equipment and fences repaired. She also got support from local law enforcement officials to patrol the school grounds so that adults would no longer use them as places to congregate. Some principals enlist students in the continuing effort to keep school facilities clean and attractive. With assistance from teachers and talented community members, students can decorate hallways with murals and other artwork. An attractive environment sends a clear message that people care about a school.

Instructional materials. It is difficult for teachers to teach and students to learn when they lack textbooks, technology, and other instructional materials. Cutting through the red tape of purchasing departments requires school leaders to work closely with school district leaders. When district funds are unavailable to acquire instructional materials, principals may need to appeal to local organizations and businesses. Examples abound of school-community partnerships that provide low-performing schools with everything from computers to library books. The acquisition of up-to-date equipment, textbooks, software, and other materials, as in the case of improvements to school facilities, can be of enormous symbolic value to students and teachers. Knowing that people care about a school and those who study and teach in it serves as a vital source of hope.

Schedule adjustments. Another area where "quick wins" are possible is the school's daily schedule. Schedule adjustments may be needed for various reasons. If literacy is the focus of turnaround efforts, for example, students need to be exposed to instruction in reading, writing, and related subjects for large blocks of time each day. Allington (2006) contends, "A good first principle in organizing a school more efficiently is to provide every classroom with at least two and one-half hours of uninterrupted time [for language arts]—no pull-outs, no push-ins, no specials" (p. 50). When researchers (Le Floch et al., 2007) investigated elementary schools "in improvement" under the No Child Left Behind Act, they found that almost one-third of them had increased time on reading by more than 30 minutes a day in order to raise achievement (p. 93). Additional reading time may best be spent with students receiving instruction in small reading groups.

By implementing some form of parallel block schedule, elementary principals can facilitate small-group instruction in reading (Canady & Rettig, 2008). Parallel block schedules make it possible for more professional staff—not just homeroom teachers—to participate in reading groups for a portion of each day. By engaging teachers of noncore subjects, media specialists, and other specialists in reading instruction and using "extension centers" for large-group instruction, parallel block schedules can increase opportunities for small-group instruction, thereby providing needy students with more individual attention.

Another reason for adjusting the daily schedule is to provide time for tutoring and other forms of assistance for struggling students. Some school turnaround initiatives rely on extending the regular school day, while others offer before-school tutorials or Saturday programs (Le Floch et al., 2007, p. 92). The viability of these arrangements, of course, may depend on the availability of transportation for students who come early or stay late to get extra help. Another option that has been successful involves setting aside time at the end of the regular school day for teachers to reteach students who had trouble with the day's lessons. Classmates who do not require additional help are provided with opportunities for academic enrichment.

A third reason to adjust the daily schedule is to provide teachers with opportunities to meet during the regular school day. Meetings may be devoted to planning, curriculum coordination, and analyzing student achievement data. While time for teachers to meet also can be created by hiring substitutes, having administrators cover class, and releasing students early one day a week, the preferred arrangement involves building meeting time into the regular school schedule. One North Carolina elementary school, for example, created "block planning time" by scheduling special classes for equal periods of instruction on a rotating schedule during the same time block one day per week (Bingham, Harman, & Embree, 1997). Students at the same grade level experience varying sequences of physical education, music, and media for 30 minutes each, providing 90 minutes of shared planning time for their three classroom teachers.

Regardless of whether school leaders adjust the daily schedule, acquire new computers, or spruce up school facilities, they must cultivate close working relationships with central office personnel. Achieving "quick wins" depends on knowing people who are in a position to expedite requests and who understand the importance of timely action when it comes to achieving school turnarounds.

Confidence Building

Years of teaching in a low-performing school can undermine teachers' confidence and sense of efficacy. Successful turnaround specialists understand the necessity of taking actions to raise the self-efficacy of individual faculty members as well as boost the collective efficacy of the entire faculty. Two keys to this process are teamwork and training.

No educator, however capable, can turn around a low-performing school alone. In schools that have been low performing for awhile, teachers often work in isolation. They rarely collaborate to share ideas, discuss struggling students, and plan improvements.

Teamwork begins at the top. Principals should model the importance of teamwork by creating a leadership team to assist in the process of diagnosing conditions in need of improvement and guiding the school turnaround process. At the elementary level, leadership teams may consist of the principal, grade-level representatives, a special education teacher, a reading specialist, and a guidance counselor.

Another type of team involves all the staff members who serve students at a particular grade level. Besides classroom teachers, grade-level teams can include teachers of special subject such as physical education and music, special education teachers, reading specialists, and paraprofessionals. Grade-level teams assume responsibility for aligning the curriculum with state and local standards, analyzing student performance on formative and summative assessments, coordinating lessons, organizing reading groups, and providing assistance to struggling students.

A good example of how a grade-level team operates comes from a case study of Principal Paula Frazier's efforts to turn around Pleasant Valley Elementary School in Rockingham County, Virginia (Frazier & Salmonowicz, 2006):

> We analyze our test results each year, question by question. . . . We look at the lowest five questions in each of the core subjects . . . and that becomes part of our annual school plan. And then we come up with activities, ways to assess each of those questions and topics. I consider it the science of teaching—breaking components down and determining where we are and where we need to go. (p. 4)

To ensure that the curriculum content at each grade level is articulated, teachers from different grade levels also need to work together. Vertical teams of teachers should be formed to review instructional objectives and lesson content on a periodic basis. When students at one grade level fail to perform well in a particular subject, members of a vertical team must consider whether the students were not exposed to important content at the previous grade level. Vertical teams also can assist in the process of assigning students to teachers at succeeding grade levels.

Other types of teams include school improvement teams, special education teams, and crisis management teams. By shifting some responsibil-. ity for student performance from individuals to teams, principals promote a spirit of cooperation and reduce feelings of isolation.

Confidence is a function of competence. Teachers can develop competence by sharing with each other in various kinds of teams. They also can acquire competence through staff and professional development activities. In dozens of case studies of successful school turnarounds, virtually every case involves additional training for teachers—but not just any training. Staff and professional development must target specific areas of need, such as the implementation of a new reading program, how to analyze student test data, and strategies for differentiating instruction. In order to turn around Berkeley Elementary School in central Virginia, Catherine Thomas realized that her teachers, many of whom were in their first or second year of teaching, lacked extensive knowledge of the reading process and how to diagnose reading problems (Duke et al., 2005). Rather than arrange several "drive-by workshops," she used Title I funds to organize a yearlong series of trainings on how to implement Berkeley's new reading series. The same consultant provided all the training, thereby ensuring continuity of content and familiarity with the challenges faced by Berkeley teachers.

When veteran teachers are involved, staff and professional development activities are unlikely to be effective unless and until teachers carefully examine their current practice. Opportunities must be available to identify and question well-established routines associated with planning, instructional delivery, and classroom assessment (Duke, 2004, pp. 124–130). Principals, however, should appreciate how difficult it can be for many veteran teachers to admit that their methods may need to be changed. The more principals can do to encourage and even reward reflection and honest self-assessment, the more likely teachers will embrace the value of continuous improvement.

More Time-Consuming Initiatives

Much of the work of school leaders discussed up to this point can be undertaken during the first months of the school turnaround process. In fact, if a direction is not set, if several "quick wins" are not achieved, and if teamwork and training are not developed in the initial phase of school turnaround, the likelihood of ultimate success is greatly reduced (Herman et al., 2008). Other initiatives, however, may require more time, perhaps as much as a semester or more. These initiatives include curriculum alignment, staffing, and instructional interventions.

Curriculum alignment. Ensuring that students are taught content that aligns with local and state curriculum guidelines and state standardized tests requires considerable effort and oversight. An increasing number of school districts are addressing curriculum alignment on a systemwide basis. Teams of teachers from all grade levels are enlisted to develop lessons based on curriculum guidelines and uniform instructional objectives. Pacing guides may be used to make certain that all of the required content is covered during the school year.

Where curriculum alignment is undertaken at the district level, the task of the school turnaround specialist is to make sure that teachers actually use the aligned lessons and that students master the required instructional objectives. In some cases, however, no districtwide curriculum alignment initiative has been undertaken. Under such circumstances, principals of low-performing schools must organize faculty members to accomplish the task. Work on curriculum alignment often is deferred until the summer, when teachers have large blocks of time to devote to it. Teachers, of course, must be reimbursed for their efforts when it entails noncontractual time. When no prior effort has been made to undertaken curriculum alignment, it may be necessary to begin with one or two subjects. The logical candidates for initial alignment efforts are English/language arts and mathematics.

Staffing. Many school leaders admit that the hardest part of turning around a low-performing school involves staffing issues. Sometimes the issue concerns moving teachers to a different assignment. In other cases, the issue entails documenting a poorly qualified teacher and taking the steps necessary to replace the individual. A national assessment of Title I programs (Stullich, Eisner, & McCrary, 2007) reported that teachers in low-performing schools were less likely to be "highly qualified" than teachers in other schools (p. 77). Recruiting and retaining capable teachers and acquiring additional staff members constitute other staffing challenges.

If a school has failed to make adequate yearly progress for a number of years, it may need to be reconstituted. Under this sanction, faculty members have to reapply for their positions. Reapplication provides the principal, who is likely to be newly appointed, with an opportunity to select only the teachers who have the competence and the commitment to help struggling students. Filling vacant positions, however, may not be easy. Superintendents can help by allowing school turnaround specialists to have the first choice of teacher applicants for district teaching positions. Long-term substitute teachers sometimes may be needed until a highly qualified candidate can be located.

The school turnaround process in most cases begins before reconstitution is called for. In these instances, principals must start off by assessing faculty strengths and weaknesses and redeploying teachers who are in positions where their skills are not well utilized (Herman et al., 2008, p. 28). It is crucial that the strongest instructors have opportunities to work with the weakest students. Turnaround specialists sometimes report that they have a few teachers who are unable or unwilling to make the adjustments necessary to contribute to the turnaround process. These teachers must be observed, placed on plans of assistance, and replaced if they fail to meet the conditions spelled out in the plans. Such actions require the backing of the superintendent and can take as long as an entire school year. In the meantime, principals must see that the teachers are assigned in ways that minimize their negative impact on student learning.

Another staffing issue involves acquiring additional staff. Principals charged with turning around low-performing schools frequently express the need for an additional reading specialist or a mathematics specialist. Once again, the support of the superintendent is needed to secure more faculty.

The availability of specialists enables principals to develop new staffing arrangements better suited to the needs of struggling students. Low reading groups, for example, may be staffed by a classroom teacher and a reading specialist. Special education teachers and regular education teachers can work in tandem in order to implement meaningful inclusion programs. Specialists also can provide on-site training for classroom teachers.

Instructional interventions. When teachers routinely reteach subject matter that students have difficulty understanding, they reduce the need for special instructional interventions. Still, there are likely to be students who will need additional help beyond what they receive in their regular classes. It may take a turnaround specialist several months to determine the best ways to arrange interventions. Sometimes, the daily schedule is organized so that students in need of assistance can receive it on a "pull-out" basis. In other cases, intervention specialists enter classes and work directly with students during their lessons. Many school turnaround initiatives include extended day programs in which students spend additional time at school in the afternoon. When Harry Reasor, the principal of a Grade 5–8 school in Pennington Gap, Virginia, launched a school turnaround initiative, he found that it was more effective to assign students to the extended day program on an "as needed" basis than to insist that they stay after regular school hours every afternoon. Assistance was targeted to specific instructional objectives with which individual students were struggling.

Getting students to perform better on state standardized tests is an important part of the school turnaround process. In order for students to be well-prepared for these tests, some principals schedule intensive review sessions just before state tests are administered. These review sessions may be offered during the regular school day or after school. While volunteers sometimes are enlisted to help students review, there is no substitute for the involvement of students' regular teachers in test preparation activities.

Intervention programs need not be limited to academic assistance. In some low-performing schools, struggling students are perceived to need help with motivation, self-esteem, and personal responsibility.

Supplemental programs operated with the help of guidance counselors, teachers, and community volunteers can provide students with the emotional support and study skills to succeed academically.

Summer provides additional opportunities for interventions. Some programs are designed to give low-performing students a head start on the next school year's work. When Mark Keeler, principal of South River Elementary School in Rockingham County, Virginia, realized that his rising fifth graders were particularly weak in their reading skills, he arranged for a "jumpstart" summer program to enable fifth-grade teachers to build relationships with their incoming students and identify areas of academic need. Other types of summer programs try to keep students reading and prevent loss of learning over the summer break.

No matter what the intervention, school leaders need to make certain that periodic evaluations are conducted to determine whether the intervention is effective. Continuing to operate interventions that fail to make an impact constitutes a waste of valuable time and resources. Successful turnaround specialists continually assess interventions and consider alternative sources of assistance that might be more effective.

SCHOOL TURNAROUND LEADERSHIP

School leaders charged with turning around low-performing schools face a set of challenges that differ in important ways from those school leaders hoping to prevent schools from slipping into decline. While prevention is the focus of the latter, intervention is the central concern for the former. Turnaround specialists understand that there are too many problems in a low-performing school to address all of them simultaneously. Energies and resources must be focused on a relatively narrow set of priorities, and the number-one priority in many cases involves literacy instruction. Improvements in reading, writing, and related aspects of literacy are keys to improvements elsewhere.

Raising student achievement in literacy demands the commitment of all staff members. Commitment, in turn, depends on staff members possessing the confidence to examine their practice and explore new ways of teaching and working together. Successful turnaround specialists know that achieving a few "quick wins" right off the bat can spur confidence and build the momentum needed to tackle greater challenges. "Quick wins" may involve improvements to school facilities, reducing behavior and attendance problems, and adjusting the daily schedule to make it possible for teachers to plan together. Teamwork and advanced training can serve as additional sources of confidence. Eventually, school leaders must also ensure that the curriculum is aligned to state standards and tests, personnel issues are resolved, and effective interventions to help struggling students are put in place.

KEY LESSONS AND NEXT STEPS

A number of lessons can be learned from studies of "school turnaround specialists" like Wilma Williams. These lessons include the following:

- No matter how bad off a school is, the situation can get worse if the principal fails to exercise good judgment.
- To turn around a low-performing school, a principal must provide a clear sense of direction and inspire widespread commitment to it.
- Selecting a focus for the early stages of the turnaround process invariably entails trade-offs.
- All faculty members should be engaged in teaching literacy.
- Teamwork and training can boost teacher confidence and competence, thereby enabling teachers to tackle the turnaround process.

Turnaround for a low-performing school is just the first step in a prolonged process of school improvement. For Wilma Williams, the next steps involved these actions:

- The new reading program and interventions for struggling students need to be evaluated on an ongoing basis to determine if they are effective.
- Training for teachers in literacy instruction and instructional interventions must be provided on a continuing basis in order to reinforce key concepts and introduce newly hired teachers to core programs.
- Teachers who fail to implement the new reading program effectively need to be replaced.
- Instruction has to be monitored to ensure that what is being taught is aligned with state and district curriculum guidelines.
- Teachers' teams should be observed to make certain that planning time is being used productively.

PART III

The Challenge of Sustaining School Improvement

Turning around a low-performing school is one kind of leadership challenge; keeping the school turned around is quite another. Sustaining success on the surface seems so simple. Just keep on doing whatever was done to achieve initial improvements. As it turns out, there's more to sustaining success than merely maintaining the original course of action. Evidence suggests that initial increases in student achievement often level off or even reverse themselves. Premature celebration, fatigue, and complacency can contribute to loss of momentum. Circumstances change as key staff members leave, resources are re-directed elsewhere, and new students arrive. The leadership needed to keep a school moving forward requires attention to a set of additional concerns quite distinct from those that had to be addressed initially to turn the school around.

5

Reversing School Failure Is Only the First Step

A PROMISING START AT STUART HIGH SCHOOL*

Looking back over his first years as principal of J. E. B. Stuart High School in Fairfax County, Virginia, Principal Mel Riddile had to feel reasonably satisfied. When he took over in 1997, the former "yuppy school" had become a highly diverse high school of 1,500 students. No ethnic or racial groups predominated. Stuart's student body was made up of Hispanic (40%), Asian (21%), Middle Eastern (14%), Caucasian (12%), African American (10%), and "other" (3%) students. Half of the students qualified for free or reduced-price lunch. Acts of violence, gang activity, and discipline problems at and near the school raised parents' concerns for the safety of their children. The average SAT score of 951 was the lowest of any high school in Fairfax County. Of 11 state Standards of Learning tests administered for the first time in 1998, Stuart students had achieved an adequate passing rate for only one test. Student attendance stood at 89 percent, well below the school system average of 95 percent.

---

*Information for this case was derived from personal communication with Principal Mel Riddile, a case study by Dorothy Kelly that is part of the Darden Graduate School of Business Administration collection of case students (UVA-OB-0853), and an article by Carol Guensburg entitled "Reading Rules" and published in *Edutopia*, vol. 2, no. 1 (February 2006), pp. 40–42.

By 2000, Stuart High School was well on its way to improved performance. Students had achieved acceptable passing rates in eight of the state's 11 Standards of Learning tests. Attendance, SAT scores, and graduation rates were on the rise, and safety concerns were diminishing. Stuart High School clearly had begun to turn around.

What had enabled these early gains to be made? Like Wilma Williams in the previous section, Riddile understood that a large portion of Stuart's students were unlikely to raise their overall academic performance unless the faculty focused on literacy. And that meant all faculty members, not just English teachers. After administering reading tests to Stuart students, the lowest readers were assigned to reading teachers for one-on-one instruction. Riddile hired a reading coach to work with the entire faculty on ways to address reading in various subject matter areas.

Riddile simultaneously zeroed in on attendance problems. Students were unlikely to improve their academic performance if they frequently missed school. He launched a major campaign to reduce absenteeism. A phone call was made to the home of every student who was absent. Parents were encouraged to make certain that their children got to school on time.

A foundation for academic success definitely had been laid, but Riddile understood that early accomplishments could be reversed if additional steps were not taken. As he surveyed the unfinished agenda, Riddile pinpointed several areas needing attention. The organizational structure of Stuart, as with any other typical high school, was not well suited to providing intensive assistance to weak readers. The school calendar, limited to 180 days of instruction, did not help the cause. Some students were so far behind that they needed additional time if they ever were to catch up to their peers.

Developing better readers, Riddile realized, was a means to an end not an end in itself. In order to benefit from a high school education, students needed to do well in various academic areas. They needed to be challenged if they were to succeed in a highly competitive environment like Fairfax County. Just passing state standardized tests would not be enough. Some teachers, however, doubted that many of Stuart's students were capable of meeting more rigorous expectations. Riddile was especially concerned about the students in special education and the English language learners.

DETERMINING THE UNFINISHED AGENDA

As anyone who has ever tried to lose weight or quit smoking can attest, sustaining initial success is no easy matter. Those who study organizational change long have recognized that promising improvements cannot be maintained without a great deal of planning and effort. When Elmore (2007) investigated an improving elementary and middle school, he found that their performance went "flat" after initial gains. Unsurprised by this development, he explained that early jumps in student achievement can be obtained by having teachers (1) spend more time on key subjects such as reading and mathematics and (2) focus on helping students who are close to passing standardized tests (p. 248). Sustaining success is more challenging, though, because all the "low-hanging fruit" already has been picked.

Fullan (2001) noted a phenomenon similar to Elmore's flattened performance. After an initial phase of dramatic improvement, Fullan found that improving schools can experience an "implementation dip" (p. 40). Whatever changes had produced early gains—new policies, programs, and/or practices—over time became vulnerable to less rigorous implementation efforts. Be it reform fatigue, the introduction of new mandates, or preoccupation with other matters, the individuals responsible for implementing reforms seemed in many cases to lose focus and momentum.

In our experience at the University of Virginia, many of the schools participating in the School Turnaround Program saw their test scores drop in the second year, after experiencing impressive improvements in year one. The causes of these unexpected U-turns were not always apparent. In some cases, premature celebration and subsequent complacency seemed to be factors. When our turnaround specialists remained at the helm and made appropriate adjustments, however, test scores often started rising again in the third year.

Maintaining momentum is a challenge for any school leader who gets off to a promising start with an initiative designed to raise performance. The sense of urgency that frequently is associated with initial improvements cannot be sustained indefinitely. At the same time, expectations rarely remain constant. Many accountability systems, including those that derive from the No Child Left Behind Act, have provisions for steadily rising benchmarks. Maintaining last year's performance is not good enough. School leaders are faced with a continuing need to boost achievement.

Many of the challenges that can undermine leadership for sustained improvement are predictable. They include (1) ensuring continuity, (2) coping with complexity, (3) moving beyond basics, (4) addressing the needs of underperforming groups, and (5) detecting weaknesses in school culture. Let us look more closely at each of these concerns.

Ensuring Continuity

Turning around a low-performing school is all about *change*, but sustaining the turnaround can have a lot to do with *continuity*. Many of the factors contributing to early improvements must be maintained if schools are to avoid slippage.

Leadership tops the list. As the previous section indicated, turning around a low-performing school requires exceptional leadership. Principals must carefully assess the conditions associated with low performance, identify priorities, and mobilize support to tackle the priorities. Such work demands school leaders who are prepared to provide a high level of direction. Once student achievement begins to improve, however, a high level of direction may become counterproductive. Teachers can grow resentful of principals who continue to insist on closely supervising all aspects of school operations. Such leadership often is interpreted as a lack of trust in the capabilities of faculty members.

School turnarounds depend on collaboration and teamwork, and it is hard to imagine sustaining improvements without continued collaboration and teamwork. The effort to achieve early gains, however, can leave teachers and other staff members exhausted. The first year of school turnaround typically involves frequent meetings, new committees, lots of collective planning and data analysis, focused staff development, and longer hours. Maintaining such an intense pace can lead to frustration and burnout.

Sustaining teamwork presents additional problems, especially for teachers who are used to working alone. While teacher teams can produce impressive results, they often come at a cost. Working with colleagues increases the likelihood of interpersonal tensions and disagreements. Just like a successful marriage, successful teams demand considerable energy and attention. Team members are quick to sense any lack of effort by certain team members. By the second year of teaming, some teachers may long for the simplicity and relative freedom of working in isolation.

School turnarounds usually are characterized by the creation of new programs to address the needs of struggling learners. Principals express great pride when they are able to develop programs that contribute to improved instruction and remediation. Problems arise, though, when it comes to maintaining these programs. Principals often expect to hand off program supervision to someone else once a new program is up and running. What they sometimes discover, however, is that the new program manager lacks the competence or the commitment to maintain the program properly. The once promising program consequently suffers neglect and declining effectiveness. Those associated with the program feel their valuable time has been for naught. They are less likely to support future program development.

A fourth aspect of school turnarounds where continuity is crucial concerns resources. Principals typically are given access to additional resources in order to launch a turnaround initiative. These resources may include special district funding, grants from foundations, and local partnerships. The extra funds enable schools to provide staff and professional development, acquire new materials and equipment, and hire additional staff members. Once the school begins to improve, however, these additional resources may disappear or be redirected to more needy schools. The result can be stalled improvement and feelings of abandonment on the part of school staff members.

Coping With Complexity

It is not unreasonable for teachers in a low-performing school to expect that school turnaround efforts ultimately will result in better performance and less ambiguity and confusion. The hope is held out that "working smarter" will lead to not having to "work harder." What teachers frequently discover, though, is that improvement initiatives produce more, not less, organizational complexity.

Elmore (2007) characterizes the period immediately following the initial turnaround as a "very tricky stage" in which the "problems of improvement become more complex and demanding as performance increases" (p. 251). He goes on to observe,

> Often schools go through some kind of crisis at around this time, where teachers and principals argue that the work has become impossible to do under existing resource constraints and that expectations set by external accountability systems are simply impossible to meet. (Ibid.)

Greater organizational complexity, as noted earlier, is associated with more committees, more meetings, more planning, and more responsibilities. Though justified in terms of the promise of greater instructional effectiveness, these changes actually may appear to reduce the time available for teaching and learning. Such conditions cause staff members to question the benefits of school improvement efforts. A collective desire to return to the ways things used to be often arises under such circumstances, presenting school leaders with a considerable challenge.

Complexity and confusion frequently go hand in hand. Turning around a low-performing school can produce new structural arrangements, such as school improvement teams, vertical and horizontal groups of teachers, and instructional intervention teams. The proliferation of new organizational entities sometimes leads to confusion regarding reporting relationships and sources of authority. Is the school's instructional intervention team, for example, ultimately responsible for providing assistance to a struggling student? Is it the student's teacher? Is it the teacher's grade-level team? Does the newly created *School Improvement Team* trump the long-standing *Faculty Senate*? School leaders frequently are so busy during the early stages of the school turnaround process that they neglect to develop clear understandings of lines of authority and reporting relationships. Such circumstances can inhibit any effort to sustain initial improvements.

Moving Beyond Basics

Improving students' skills related to literacy is a logical starting place for many school improvement efforts. So too are campaigns to reduce absenteeism. Eventually, though, school leaders like Mel Riddile understand that improvements in reading, writing, and attendance are means to an end, not ends in and of themselves. The real ends of sustained school improvements involve better overall academic performance, greater student motivation, lower retention rates, fewer dropouts, and more high school graduates.

Critics of contemporary educational accountability measures express fear that educators will concentrate too much on getting students to pass state-mandated standardized tests. Some of the possible negative consequences of such single-mindedness were identified in an essay by Duke, Grogan, and Tucker (2003):

> If tests stress a limited range of thinking skills and knowledge . . . they may cause teachers to deemphasize other important learning opportunities. If students far below the established cut score receive little attention because teachers feel they must concentrate their limited time and energy on helping students who are within a few points of passing, the school experiences of our most needy young people will suffer. (p. 204)

The researchers went on to raise additional concerns about the impact on highly talented students of too great a focus on standardized tests. They noted that bright students could grow restless and frustrated if they were compelled to bide their time while teachers focused on getting low-achieving students to master test material. Yet another fear expressed in their essay involved the possibility that teachers might begin to regard their students more as numbers on state tests than human beings with hopes, dreams, anxieties, and feelings.

Evidence that school turnaround efforts can stall when school leaders continue to focus exclusively on getting students to pass standardized tests is contained in the findings of a study of Chicago's high school restructuring plan. In 1997, Chicago enlisted the help of nine external partners in order to raise academic achievement in 33 high schools that were on some form of probation. When the Center for Urban School Policy at Northwestern University assessed the progress of this initiative in 2000, it found that the external partners "increasingly focused on reading, and boosting test scores in lieu of offering general staff development and professional development tailored to teachers' needs in individual schools" (Woestehoff & Neill, 2007, p. 16). The bottom line was disappointingly modest test-score gains in most of the high schools.

Chicago elementary and middle schools, as well as high schools, experienced the negative efforts of "test-centered schooling." O'Day (2002) identified several reasons why the heavy emphasis on passing state tests worked against sustained school improvements in Chicago. First, school leaders concentrated less on student learning than avoiding probation and sanctions imposed by the central administration. Students were constantly subjected to intensive drill and practice on test items. Test prep books developed by the school system replaced the regular curriculum. Even though the state tests represented relatively minimal learning requirements, teachers were reluctant to expose students to more advanced content for fear of detracting from test preparation.

The second reason why test-centeredness contributed to stalled progress, according to O'Day, involved the practice of triaging students. Students who were closest to passing state tests, based on their performance on interim tests, tended to receive the most attention, leaving to languish students judged by their teachers to be too far behind to pass the tests. Though an understandable practice in light of the heavy emphasis on test performance, triaging is hardly consistent with the mission of public education.

Addressing Under-Performing Groups

A turnaround school cannot continue to improve if it leaves some groups of students behind. Triaging students may help schools attain acceptable passing rates on state tests and thereby avoid sanctions, but it leaves highly needy students in precarious circumstances. Left unassisted, these students become prime candidates for dropping out of school. Since graduation rates now are examined as part of educational accountability systems, high schools eventually will pay the price for triaging students in elementary and middle schools.

After his early success, Mel Riddile took a close look at the achievement of various student subgroups at Stuart High School. He noticed that African American students, English language learners, and students with disabilities were still performing less well in reading and mathematics than other subgroups. There would be no sustained improvement at Stuart until interventions were developed to address the needs of these students.

Another group that may not necessarily benefit from initial school turnaround initiatives are high-achieving students. As noted earlier, it is certainly conceivable that increased attention to the needs of low-achieving students will result in diminished efforts to challenge high-achievers. In analyzing test results, school leaders must be careful to track the progress of students who previously performed at the top of their class. If the percentage of high-achieving students drops, even as the scores of low-achievers improve, efforts must be made to address the needs of high-achievers. The consequences of school improvement efforts should never include academic regression on the part of bright students.

In order to better serve underperforming student subgroups, leaders may need to confront dysfunctional school cultures. Such cultures are characterized by beliefs that certain students are unlikely to perform well in school. Unless such beliefs are addressed directly, the likelihood of sustained school improvement is slight.

Detecting Cultural Weaknesses

Schools have distinctive cultures and subcultures. It takes years for cultures to develop. The culture of a school is unlikely, therefore, to be completely changed in the early stages of school improvement. Reculturing a school is, by definition, a long-term process. Nonetheless, school leaders intent on sustaining early successes must diagnose weaknesses in the existing school culture and engage in efforts to correct them.

One weakness was noted in the preceding section—the belief that some students are incapable of meeting high expectations. Such a belief can become a self-fulfilling prophecy. So too can the belief that veteran teachers are too set in their ways to change their instructional practice and the belief that poor parents are uninterested in getting involved in their children's schooling.

Despite the fact that organizational culture is an abstract concept, it does not take a visitor long to detect aspects of a school's culture. Culture is conveyed in the way staff members think of themselves, their colleagues, and their work. It is embodied in assumptions about students and parents, beliefs about teaching and learning, and values regarding what it means to be an educator. Maehr and Midgley (1996) maintain that the only way to effect changes in school culture is to alter the way people think, including how school leaders, teachers, and students think about their roles, responsibilities, and capabilities (p. 201).

Research on cognitive change remains inconclusive. In some cases, beliefs must change before behavior changes. In other cases, people change their behavior first, and if the behavior produces desired results, then beliefs eventually change. In either instance, change is unlikely to occur overnight.

An improvement in student achievement on one year's standardized tests is no guarantee that school culture has changed completely. Though no longer toxic, the school culture may have become merely benign. Under such circumstances, school personnel attribute improvements to luck, a unique cohort of students, or exceptionally great effort on the part of staff members. Left unchanged are fundamental beliefs about what certain students are capable of and what the role of teacher should entail. The school culture, in other words, is still not thought to be an active contributor to sustained success.

The cultures of schools that have been low-performing for a long time often are characterized by widespread distrust. Teachers distrust parents and school leaders. School leaders distrust teachers and central office supervisors. Parents distrust school personnel. Students distrust teachers. Such widespread distrust may not disappear simply because a school launches an improvement process and test scores begin to rise. The initiation of reforms, in fact, may only exacerbate distrust. Hargreaves and Fink (2006) have observed, "If truth is the first casualty of war, then trust is the first fatality of imposed reform" (p. 212). Teachers, for example, may interpret the imposition of a school turnaround program as evidence that school leaders do not trust their professional competence and judgment. For their part, teachers believe that they are working as hard as they can and doing a reasonably good job under adverse circumstances.

In her research on novice teachers, Johnson (2004) found that one of the factors that determined whether a new teacher remained in the profession was the culture of the school in which he or she first taught. Low-performing schools often employ a high percentage of new teachers since the turnover rate tends to be high and capable veterans seek positions in more successful schools. This means that there is a greater likelihood that freshly minted teachers will be exposed to dysfunctional school cultures. Sustained school improvement depends on retaining capable and energetic young teachers. School leaders cannot afford to lose these teachers because they find their school's culture to be uninviting and defeatist.

MEETING THE CHALLENGE OF SUSTAINED IMPROVEMENT

School leaders with extensive experience in turning around low-performing schools understand that raising student achievement in a given year is not cause for declaring victory. Early gains easily can disappear if school leaders ignore the factors that contribute to long-term success. One such factor involves maintaining momentum. The first year of school improvement can leave faculty members feeling exhausted and students feeling overtested. Programs initiated in the first year of a turnaround project must be nurtured and fine-tuned, resources must be secured for succeeding years, and teachers must be persuaded not to revert to old patterns of behavior. Another factor involves coping with the complexity that invariably accompanies school improvement efforts, complexity exemplified by more committees, more meetings, more planning, and more responsibilities.

School turnarounds also can stall when teachers insist on focusing exclusively on getting students to pass standardized tests covering the "basics." These tests may be required for purposes of educational accountability, but they do little to motivate students to excel or prepare students for the challenges awaiting them after graduation.

It is not uncommon for some student subgroups to experience relatively few benefits from the early stages of school improvement. These subgroups can range from students with disabilities to high achievers. Sustaining school improvement depends on ensuring that all students share in the benefits of academic reforms.

The last factor that can derail school improvement involves school culture. School leaders should not assume that initial gains in achievement, however impressive, constitute proof that school culture has been altered.

School culture only changes when people's thinking changes, and such changes are invariably time-consuming and difficult.

KEY LESSONS AND NEXT STEPS

Efforts by leaders like Mel Riddile to turn around chronically low-performing schools can stall unless the following lessons are learned and appropriate adjustments are made:

- Early gains in achievement can disappear when initial momentum wanes, and schools settle back in to former patterns of operation.
- Teachers frequently are exhausted after the first year of school improvement.
- While school turnaround is all about change, sustaining school turnaround requires continuity.
- Teachers may question the value of turnaround initiatives if they are perceived to reduce time for classroom instruction.
- Improving literacy is a means to an end, not an end in itself.

Faced with the need to consolidate and sustain early gains, principals of improving schools should consider the following steps:

- Attention must be devoted to upgrading the entire curriculum, not just content related to literacy and mathematics.
- The school's capacity for helping all students, not just those who are close to passing standardized tests, has to be increased.
- A concerted effort should be made to develop a constructive school culture that supports continuous improvement.
- Provisions are needed to ensure the ongoing recruitment, retention, and development of highly qualified staff members.

6

Leadership to Sustain School Improvement

M el Riddile had provided the leadership necessary to arrest Stuart
High School's declining performance and start the school on an
upward trajectory, but he also understood that a somewhat different kind
of leadership would be required if early progress was to be sustained.
Continuing to focus on literacy and school safety might prevent Stuart
from slipping back, but it would do little to offer students the kind of high-
quality education they would need to land good jobs and get into competitive colleges. Every principal has some sense of what they are and are
not capable of accomplishing. In Mel Riddile's case, he felt confident that
he could make the necessary adjustments in his leadership to take Stuart
to the next level.

Whereas turning around a low-performing school entails generating a
sense of urgency and acting quickly and decisively to initiate highly
focused change, sustaining school improvement calls for more measured
steps designed for the long haul. Elmore (2004) notes, "The problems of
improvement become more complex and demanding as performance
increases; the challenges to existing instructional practices and existing
organizational norms, more direct and difficult" (p. 251). The concerns
raised in Chapter 5—concerns that include the challenges of culture, complexity, and continuity—must be addressed along with a host of additional
issues. These additional issues range from resolving staffing problems to
fine-tuning interventions to distributing leadership among staff members.

Leadership for sustained improvement is all about building school capacity. Capacity is a function of the competence and commitment of staff members, the organizational structure within which they work, the values and beliefs that characterize the school's culture, the range of options available to students to ensure their continued growth, and the quality of assistance provided students who continue to struggle. This chapter examines what school leaders need to do in order to build capacity for long-term success.

BUILDING CAPACITY FOR SUSTAINED SUCCESS

KEY QUESTIONS

1. What can be done to extend the focus of school improvement beyond curriculum basics?

2. How can a school's capacity for helping all students be refined?

3. What steps can school leaders take to develop a culture of continuous improvement?

4. What can school leaders do to recruit, develop, and retain a highly qualified faculty?

Solidifying Early Gains at Stuart High

Before taking a closer look at each of the key questions, it is instructive to examine what Mel Riddile and his staff did to maintain momentum in their effort to make Stuart High School one of the best high schools in Fairfax County.

Riddile realized that Stuart's location ensured that the student body for the foreseeable future would consist of a broad range of students, including English language learners, recently arrived immigrants, and high-achievers who expected to attend good colleges. The conventional structure of Stuart High School, he concluded, was ill suited to the needs of such a highly diverse population. In order to accommodate all of Stuart's students, Riddile decided that the high school should be subdivided into three distinct units. In effect, he created three schools where previously there had been one.

The first school was developed to serve the needs of the approximately 400 students who knew little or no English. This school functioned a lot like an elementary school, with students spending most of each day with the same one or two teachers. The primary focus of instruction was reading and language skills. Instructional materials included the kinds of picture books, basal readers, and wall displays typically found in primary classrooms.

When students developed a working knowledge of English, they transferred into what amounted to a middle school. In this setting, students moved along at their own pace. The flexible schedule enabled them to transition from one course to another whenever they reached the required competency level. It did not matter if this level was reached in October or March. Riddile did not want students who already were behind their peers to wait around until a new semester began in order to enroll in the next course needed for graduation.

The third school at Stuart constituted a regular high school. Students transferred to this school when they were proficient in English and capable of holding their own with native English speakers. To reinforce the fact that Stuart held high expectations for all students, the high school unit offered both Advanced Placement (AP) and International Baccalaureate (IB) courses to students. Enrollment was open to any student, and all students were encouraged to enroll in at least one of these challenging courses. Eventually, almost half of the 11th and 12th graders at Stuart took at least one AP or IB course.

Rearranging the structure of Stuart High School was a necessary step toward sustained success, but one that was insufficient by itself to ensure continued academic progress. To support the new structure, Riddile believed that a new school calendar was needed. Learning is a function of time. The more time that is available, the more learning that will take place. Riddile secured the superintendent's blessing along with additional district resources to enable Stuart to move from a 180-day to a 242-day school year. First, however, Riddile had to secure the support of at least 70 percent of the Stuart staff as well as parents and students. It took almost two years to convince all parties of the benefits of a longer school year. Even then, two remaining hurdles had to be cleared. Armed with signatures from supportive staff, parents, and students, Riddile went to the Fairfax School Board. They voted to support the change, contingent on approval by the state Board of Education. Despite opposition from the hospitality industry that counted on teenagers to work during the summer, Riddile secured the state board's approval.

The new school calendar included an eight-week summer trimester that allowed students who were deficient in the number of credits needed to graduate to complete two additional semester or yearlong courses. Other students were able to continue to work on courses that they had begun during the regular school year but had not yet mastered. The new summer trimester meant that students could complete five years of coursework in four calendar years. Without the new calendar, many English language learners who needed to spend their first year at Stuart developing proficiency in English would have been unable to earn a diploma.

Restructuring Stuart and changing the school calendar were not the only keys to sustained improvement. Riddile and his staff constantly tinkered with the academic program in order to ensure that all students would get the help they needed. Algebra and transitional English classes were expanded to 95 minutes in order to provide students with more instructional time. When teachers told Riddile that students were not taking advantage of voluntary afterschool help sessions, he mandated that all students receiving a *D* or *F* grade in a core subject had to attend two-hour help sessions until their grade improved. Riddile negotiated with the central office in order to get late buses for students who stayed after school to receive help. Within a few months of implementing the new mandate, low grades dropped by 50 percent.

Riddile understood that the ninth grade was a particularly difficult year for students, especially if they lacked skills in English or had fallen behind their peers in middle school. To make certain that rising ninth graders got off to a good start at Stuart, Riddile and his staff worked closely with the middle schools that sent students to Stuart. They monitored eighth-grade reading assessments and provided every ninth-grade teacher with reading proficiency data on every one of their incoming students. This data was placed in the teachers' gradebooks so they would be aware when particular students came to Stuart with reading deficiencies. Riddile expected every Stuart teacher to be responsible for teaching reading. He backed up this expectation with appropriate inservice training. A literacy coach also was hired to work with teachers in class.

Rising ninth graders with identified weaknesses in reading and other subjects were encouraged to attend a summer academy at Stuart. The academies provided an opportunity for teachers to get to know students and students to get to know the high school. Summer academy participation enabled teachers to pinpoint deficiencies in basic skills and begin corrective measures before the beginning of school in August.

Another initiative to bolster ninth-grade instruction involved reducing class sizes for all ninth-grade core courses. Riddile wanted to make certain that students who needed help had every opportunity to receive it. Getting off to a good start in the ninth grade, Riddile knew, would pay dividends later in high school.

Riddile also understood that none of the measures that were introduced to sustain improvements at Stuart would succeed without the right staff. Five years after he took the helm at Stuart, one teacher out of five still did not meet the federal definition of "highly qualified." The lack of teachers with an appropriate credential was especially great in special education classes, and the relatively low level of achievement of students with disabilities reflected it. With the help of the school system's human resource department and focused recruitment efforts by Riddile and his leadership team, the percentage of non-highly-qualified teachers was lowered to less than 2 percent by 2003.

Having highly qualified teachers, of course, is important, but only if they are assigned in ways that maximize their effectiveness. Toward this end, Riddile insisted that his strongest teachers teach courses for students who were furthest behind grade-level expectations.

The success of Riddile's efforts to maintain improvement in academic performance at Stuart High School is a matter of record. Five years after he assumed the principalship, more than 80 percent of Stuart's students passed all 11 of Virginia's required end-of-course tests. The average SAT score rose by 104 points from 951 to 1,055. School attendance stood at 96 percent. The graduation rate increased to 97 percent, and nine out of ten graduating seniors were scheduled to attend two- or four-year colleges.

The truest test of sustainability, however, may involve the fate of improvements after a successful principal leaves. Mel Riddile left Stuart in 2006. Two years after his departure, high percentages of students continued to pass end-of-course tests, earn diplomas, and attend post-secondary institutions. School attendance and participation in AP and IB courses remained at high levels. Worth noting is the fact that sustained success was accomplished despite the fact that Stuart continued to enroll large percentages of English language learners (37%), students with disabilities (15%), and students who qualified for free or reduced-price meals (58%). The mobility rate for Stuart students also remained high (22%).

Riddile's legacy perhaps is represented best in the cultural change at Stuart High School. Over the decade of Riddile's leadership, teachers learned to work collaboratively to address student needs. They acquired the skills and knowledge to handle many academic problems that previously would have been referred elsewhere. Students and faculty members no longer thought of Stuart as a low-performing school. The collective sense of pride that characterized the new culture of Stuart promised to underwrite the quest for continued success.

THE CHALLENGES OF SUSTAINED SCHOOL IMPROVEMENT

Mel Riddile and the staff of Stuart High School addressed a variety of issues in order to ensure that performance did not slip following early gains. They moved beyond the initial focus on reading to undertake improvements in the entire academic program. They expanded the school's capacity to provide help for all students who needed it. They took steps to reculture the school, and they engaged in efforts to build a staff that was prepared to tackle the challenges of sustained school improvement.

Strengthening the Entire Academic Program

The leadership needed to turn around a low-performing school frequently entails a laser-like focus on literacy. Mathematics, to a somewhat lesser extent, also receives considerable attention early in the improvement process. These two subject matter areas are keys to achievement in other academic fields, so it is only logical that they would be addressed first. They also constitute the bases for state testing programs. To sustain school improvement, however, necessitates work across the curriculum. An important step in this process involves the alignment of what is taught in various academic subjects with what is tested on state tests. These standardized tests typically reflect state curriculum guidelines. School leaders in schools that sustain success often encourage teachers to develop lesson plans that cover specific objectives tied to the state curriculum guidelines.

Though crucial, curriculum alignment is only one element in maintaining school improvement. State tests generally represent sets of relatively minimal requirements in key content areas. If teachers concentrate solely on getting students to pass state tests, students are likely to miss out on developing an in-depth understanding of the various academic subjects. It is up to school leaders, including department chairs and subject matter specialists, to see to it that students are exposed to challenging content beyond that required to pass standardized tests.

To ensure that students are exposed to challenging content in middle and high school may require a reduction in low-level courses. The adverse impact of assigning students to basic and remedial courses has been known for decades (Oakes, 1985; Weinstein, 2002). Students in these courses tend to have less positive attitudes about themselves and lower aspirations than students in honors and advanced courses. The quality of instruction in low-track classes often is questionable in part because less experienced teachers frequently are assigned to teach these classes.

Mel Riddile recognized the need for his students to aim higher academically. One response was to develop an IB program and encourage juniors and seniors to take at least one IB or AP course. Riddile's efforts were clearly in line with his superintendent's commitment to increase minority participation in top-level courses. Dan Domenech, Fairfax's superintendent, had promulgated a policy that opened enrollment in IB and AP courses to any student who wished to enroll. But he did not stop there. Domenech also instituted a policy requiring every student in an IB or AP course to take the external end-of-course exam. This policy meant that teachers had to work with *all* enrolled students, not just the ones who stood a good chance of getting a high score on the external exam.

Another way that Riddile strengthened the academic program was to make provisions for accelerated credit accumulation during the summer. He knew that many of his students needed extra time to develop proficiency in English. If there was no possibility for them to accelerate credit accumulation later on in high school, they likely would become frustrated and drop out. The intensive summer program enabled most students to graduate on time.

Yet another strategy for strengthening the academic program of an improving high school involves providing students with access to college and community college courses. Access can be achieved in various ways, ranging from distance learning and dual enrollment to actually colocating high schools and community colleges. Once student achievement in a previously low-performing high school begins to improve, it is essential that school leaders do whatever they can to facilitate student exposure to higher education opportunities. By forging cooperative arrangements with local colleges and community colleges, school leaders can give older students a taste of academic life beyond high school and increase the likelihood that students will seek to continue their education after graduation.

Prior to high school, strengthening the academic program involves exposing students to subjects in greater depth than that required to pass state tests. To make it possible for capable students to enroll in the most advanced high school courses, middle schools may need to offer courses such as Algebra I and Geometry that typically are available only in high school. Middle school principals also need to monitor elective courses to make certain that they are academically challenging.

Expanding the Capacity to Help Students

Just because a school begins to turn around is no reason to relax efforts to assist struggling students. In order to sustain early academic success, school leaders need to closely monitor efforts to provide academic help and determine if these efforts are achieving their objectives. Accomplishing this ongoing task requires a sound understanding of the conditions under which students are most likely to receive timely and targeted assistance. Five conditions are of particular importance.

Awareness constitutes the first condition. Students are unlikely to get the help they need if teachers are unaware that they are struggling. Rather than assuming that students are grasping what they are taught, teachers must frequently check to see if individual students are keeping up with the curriculum. Checking involves more than asking questions and giving quizzes to determine if students can recall what they have covered. The ultimate proof that students understand what they are learning involves being able to apply knowledge, as might be required in solving a problem or creating a product. Students can help teachers become aware of their difficulties when they feel comfortable asking for help. Teachers should be encouraged to value, reinforce, and model asking for help. Students who are able to use a computer may feel more comfortable communicating their difficulties by email than in person. Other teachers also can be a source of awareness regarding student academic issues. When teachers meet on a regular basis to share information about the students they teach, individual students are less likely to have their problems go undetected.

The second condition is understanding *why* students are struggling. Awareness, in other words, is not enough. In order to provide effective assistance, a teacher needs to have some idea of what is causing a student to struggle. Student records and discussions with the student's former teachers and guidance counselor can provide insights. So too can prolonged observations of the student at work and analyses of errors on the student's tests and assignments. In some cases, however, school leaders may need to arrange for a teacher to have access to specialists in order to diagnose the causes of academic problems. Enabling a specialist, such as a reading specialist or learning disabilities teacher, to spend time in class watching and working with a student can yield the information needed to develop an effective instructional intervention.

Competence constitutes the third condition. Understanding the reasons why a student is struggling does not necessarily mean that a teacher has the skills to deliver an effective intervention. Where such expertise is lacking, school leaders must find ways to enhance the teacher's repertoire. Staff development and university courses can be helpful, but they require time and planning. When the need for competence is immediate, the best course of action may be to retain the services of an expert who can spend time in class demonstrating how to help a struggling student.

Interventions to help struggling students range from the simple to the complex. Sometimes all that is required to get a student back on track is a change of seating, some verbal reinforcement, or a parent conference. In other cases, however, students need more sophisticated help, such as tutoring in study skills, breaking down complex learning tasks into more manageable components, and exposure to specially designed learning aids. Computer programs developed to assist students who experience difficulties learning core material increasingly are being used to supplement regular classroom instruction. School leaders should make an effort to engage teachers in developing comprehensive checklists of possible interventions that can be used as part of regular class instruction.

Competence is of little value without commitment, the fourth condition. Teachers must be committed to acquiring and using their competence to provide assistance to individual students. When teachers regard teaching as a matter of group instruction and consider individual student assistance to be the responsibility of others, such commitment is likely to be lacking. School leaders need to communicate their expectation that all teachers should be prepared to help struggling students. Referring students elsewhere for assistance must be treated only as a last resort.

The fifth and final condition associated with a school's capacity for helping students is persistence. Awareness, understanding, competence, and commitment are necessary but insufficient alone to ensure effective assistance is available to every student who needs it. Teachers must be persistent in their efforts to help. They cannot make one attempt and then move on, leaving some students to fall further and further behind their classmates. To ensure that teachers persist in their delivery of assistance, school leaders must check on struggling students on a regular basis, inquiring as to what strategies teachers are using and their effectiveness. Teacher evaluation should be based, in part, on how well teachers address the needs of struggling students.

Seeing that all teachers make an effort to help struggling students is a critical component of a school's capacity for providing timely and targeted assistance. There will be cases, however, when even the best efforts of teachers to provide assistance fail. Sustaining academic improvement, therefore, requires the development of a continuum of interventions along with measures designed to prevent learning problems from arising in the first place.

The Hartford, Connecticut, school system implemented a continuum for high school students referred to as a "pyramid of intervention" (Blankstein, 2004). At the base of the pyramid is a summer transition program designed to prepare rising at-risk ninth graders for the rigors and routines of high school. The next level of the pyramid involves the placement of every ninth and tenth grader in an interdisciplinary teaching team. Having a team of four teachers representing the core subjects work with the same group of roughly 100 students increases the likelihood that students will receive help when they first start to experience problems. There is also greater competence in a team than in any individual member of the team (pp. 239–243).

Tutored study halls serve as the third level of the pyramid of intervention. All ninth graders are required to attend tutored study halls where they receive assistance from a full-time tutor who also is a member of the interdisciplinary teaching team. Level four of the pyramid is the 15 day identification system. After the 15th day of school, each team is expected to identify all students who are falling behind and develop appropriate interventions for each student. The fifth level of intervention calls for tutors to pull struggling students out of class for focused one-on-one and small-group instruction. After-school study period is the sixth level of intervention, and students who are still experiencing difficulties are required to attend until their problems have been corrected (ibid.).

The top three levels of the pyramid consist of the credit recovery program, the Success Team, and the LIFE Program. Because Hartford high schools operate on a block schedule, all courses can be "semesterized." Students who fail to earn a half credit in the fall semester can recover that half credit in the spring semester as long as they maintain a reasonable level of effort. When none of the preceding interventions have been effective, a student may be placed in the Success Team. Parent permission is required. The Success Team provides a smaller learning environment with intensive tutorial and counseling backup. Students enter and exit the program at the beginning of each marking period. The top of the pyramid is occupied by the LIFE Program. Serving a small number of students, the LIFE Program operates as an alternative school and combines academic studies and counseling with a vocational component or service learning project (ibid.).

What is especially laudable about the Hartford pyramid is that it combines initiatives designed to *prevent* academic problems with targeted interventions just in case preventive measures do not work. Having such a continuum in place can make a significant contribution to sustaining school turnarounds. Mel Riddile's efforts at Stuart High School to identify rising ninth graders who were at-risk so they could receive special attention, place English language learners in separate classes until they acquired proficiency in English, require struggling students to attend afterschool assistance sessions, and provide credit recovery opportunities during the summer illustrate a comprehensive approach to intervention and what it can accomplish.

Reculturing the School

It is hard to imagine sustaining a turnaround initiative in a school where the culture does not undergo fundamental changes. Dysfunctional school cultures are characterized by isolation, privacy, resistance to new ideas, devotion to routines, and low expectations (Deal & Peterson, 1999; Evans-Stout, 1998). It takes more than one or two years of improving test scores to dislodge these features completely. Reculturing a school must be regarded by school leaders as ongoing work.

There is no single model of a culture capable of sustaining success, but researchers have identified a number of cultural characteristics found in many improving schools. One of these characteristics is a high level of collaboration. Teachers are willing to share responsibility for student achievement and learn from each other. Issues involving teaching and learning are discussed openly and without finger-pointing and excuse-making. Innovation and experimentation are valued.

There is much that school leaders can do to promote collaboration. The first step is to let faculty members know that collaboration is valued and expected. School leaders must examine the school schedule in order to find times when teachers can meet together on a regular basis. Assigning groups of teachers responsibilities that require collaboration is the next step. Such responsibilities range from curriculum alignment and lesson development to program evaluation and student case management. Teachers may be grouped by subject matter, grade level, or expertise. Evidence that a school's culture has embraced collaboration should not be sought in pervasive agreement on all issues but instead in a general willingness to discuss areas of disagreement in a professional manner and arrive at constructive compromises based on the best interests of students.

Another characteristic of the cultures of improving schools is a commitment to the value of continuous improvement. Teachers may express a belief in continuous improvement but fail to manifest it in their everyday activities. Routines, while a key to teacher effectiveness, can become, over the years, an excuse for resisting change. Having become comfortable with routines that initially seemed to work well, teachers sometimes fail to recognize when the routines no longer are effective or to seek new and better practices.

School leaders can promote the value of continuous improvement by helping veteran teachers identify their routines and then encouraging them to experiment with alternatives. Providing opportunities for individuals and groups of teachers to examine new research and innovative practices is another important responsibility for school leaders. Involving teachers in evaluating how well new programs have been implemented has been found to be an effective way to promote teacher growth (Manning, Sisserson, Jolliffe, Buenrostro, & Jackson, 2008). When teachers participate in determining the extent to which new practices are being adopted by their colleagues, their own understanding of these practices is enhanced. Schools that are able to sustain initial success are not "frozen in time"; they continue to evolve and fine-tune the programs, processes, and practices that led to early victories.

Besides embracing key values, successful school cultures are characterized by rituals and ceremonies endowed with symbolic importance. Few school leaders have appreciated the benefits of rituals and ceremonies more than Bruce McDade when he was principal of Manassas Park High School in northern Virginia (Duke, 2008a, pp. 113–114). Concerned that early improvements in student achievement eventually might erode, McDade, with support from his superintendent, Tom DeBolt, made certain that students and teachers regularly were reminded that their continuing target was nothing less than excellence. No sooner had ninth graders arrived at Manassas Park High School than they participated in the "Expectation of Excellence" ceremony. This "academic pep rally" provided an opportunity to honor students who had done well the preceding year and thereby set the appropriate tone for the new school year. McDade noted that schools typically end the school year with an awards ceremony. By the time the new school year begins in August, most people have forgotten about the awards, and the value of the ceremony as a motivator has been lost. The Manassas Park ceremony concludes with the announcement of "the Most Valuable Cougar," the student who best exemplifies academic excellence.

Senior Day is another ritual for Manassas Park High School. Scheduled the day before graduation, Senior Day serves as an occasion for the high school administration to acknowledge the special qualities and contributions of each and every graduate, not just the "best and the brightest." McDade's wife even made a personalized doll to present to each student, further acknowledgment that every student is known and valued as an individual.

The next day, Graduation Day, begins with each student ringing the "bell of knowledge," just as they had done when they first arrived at Manassas Park High School. In the audience at graduation are not just relatives and high school faculty but also middle school and elementary school teachers. McDade wanted to acknowledge that all teachers, not just high school teachers, contribute to each student's earning a diploma.

Teachers in Manassas Park also are recognized when they achieve tenure. While tenure in many school systems is acknowledged simply by a form letter, in Manassas Park tenure is regarded as a cause for celebration. In a public reception, the school board and superintendent, along with every principal, present each newly tenured teacher with a plaque, recognition that they have become full-fledged members of the teaching profession.

Through shared values, rituals, and ceremonies, robust school cultures remind students and teachers alike that success is possible as long as people work together and understand what is important. School cultures cannot be divorced, however, from the people who make up the school. It is to school personnel, the final piece of the sustainability puzzle, that we now turn.

Developing the Staff to Sustain Success

Low-performing schools are challenging environments in which to work. Challenges do not disappear when a low-performing school begins to turn around. It comes as no surprise that the staff turnover rate in these schools can be quite high. If early improvements in a former low-performing school are to be sustained, school leaders must find ways to develop and retain a reasonably stable staff of capable and committed professionals. Maintaining momentum is very difficult when teachers are constantly leaving, taking with them essential experience and "local knowledge."

A key element in developing a capable staff is recruitment. School leaders must be clear about the kinds of expertise needed to serve their students and then identify the places where they are most likely to find it. Schools with large numbers of English language learners from certain parts of the world, for example, have benefitted from recruiting teachers abroad. Improving schools typically involves the implementation of various reforms. To sustain these reforms requires that school leaders recruit and hire staff members who are unlikely to resist or resent these reforms. A teacher who believes that high school students should not be subjected to classes that run longer than an hour would be a poor choice for an improving high school that had made the switch to a block schedule with 90-minute periods.

In some cases, of course, expertise may be developed once teachers have been hired by providing them with opportunities for staff development and inservice training. In other cases, however, teachers who already possess specific skills should be sought. This means searching for veteran educators with an established track record. It is hard to sustain improvements with a team made up exclusively of novices. Experienced teachers are needed to guide newcomers. A capable faculty represents a balance of youthful enthusiasm and energy on one hand and experience-based wisdom and direction on the other.

School leaders who have demonstrated the ability to recruit a talented staff typically understand the value of positive working conditions. Teachers often are willing to confront daunting academic challenges if they know they will be treated as professionals. This means respecting teachers' judgments and insights and providing opportunities for teachers to participate in school decision making. Efforts to retain as well as recruit capable teachers are strengthened when prospective staff members see that teachers are able to exercise leadership. Distributing leadership opportunities to teachers has been associated with higher student achievement as well as greater teacher job satisfaction (Leithwood & Mascall, 2008).

Mel Riddile understood the link between distributed leadership and sustained success at Stuart High School. He promoted Stuart Singer, a well-respected mathematics teacher with 38 years of teaching experience at Stuart High School, to the key role of instructional coordinator. Riddile strengthened the role of department chair, assigning chairs responsibility for curriculum leadership and guiding interventions in each subject matter area. Teachers were regularly enlisted to field test and tweak new instructional strategies and interventions before recommendations were made to the entire faculty for schoolwide implementation.

Project management can be a useful vehicle for promoting distributed leadership in schools. Once improvement targets have been established in order to focus school initiatives over a designated period of time, the principal assigns a teacher or other staff member to "manage" efforts to achieve each target. Project management does not mean that a manager does all the work to achieve a target, but it does mean that this individual oversees the efforts of all staff members involved in achieving the target, monitors progress toward the target, and reports regularly on progress to the principal and fellow members of the school leadership team. Project targets can range from aligning a particular area of the curriculum with state standards to reducing student absenteeism to developing a staff development plan to promote differentiated instruction.

Induction also can be a crucial element in developing and retaining a capable staff. A carefully orchestrated induction program enables school leaders to convey clear expectations to newcomers and specify each incoming staff member's role in sustaining school success. It is important that new teachers have a clear idea of the contributions they are expected to make. They also should be informed of sources of support to which they can turn when they encounter difficulties. School leaders can bolster their induction programs by providing new teachers with access to mentors and coaches. If possible, asking recently retired teachers to return and offer guidance to their replacements can enhance the induction process. An extensive review of the literature on teacher retention concluded, "a positive hiring experience that provides a realistic job preview for new teachers and ample time to prepare for the school year is correlated with teacher satisfaction" (Johnson, Berg, & Donaldson, 2005, p. 28).

LEADERSHIP FOR THE LONG HAUL

The basic message of this chapter is that sustaining school improvements requires school leaders to attend to a particular set of organizational issues. A continuation of the leadership that achieved an initial turnaround in a low-performing school, in other words, may be insufficient to produce the conditions needed to maintain momentum. School leaders who successfully sustain and extend early gains understand the importance of going beyond a focus on curricular basics such as literacy and mathematics in order to strengthen the entire academic program. Improving reading and math skills may be necessary but insufficient alone to prepare students to compete for high quality jobs and college admission.

A focus on developing a rigorous academic program in all areas of the curriculum can backfire, however, without complementary efforts by school leaders to develop a continuum of interventions aimed at both preventing academic problems and providing timely assistance when academic problems arise. The interventions that helped to launch initial school improvement efforts need to be continually evaluated to make certain they are achieving what they were designed to achieve. Ineffective interventions should be eliminated in favor of programs that are more likely to help struggling students. Staff members need to be reminded periodically that an assistance program, no matter how carefully designed, implemented, and staffed, is not effective if it fails to correct student learning deficits. No single intervention, furthermore, is likely to be effective with every struggling student.

Sustaining school success depends a great deal on seeing that school culture becomes a constructive force in the day-to-day life of the school. School leaders must treat school reculturing as a priority, one requiring constant attention. The reculturing process entails stressing key values, such as collaboration and continuous improvement, and developing rituals and ceremonies that reinforce and celebrate these values.

Sustaining school success ultimately depends on the quality and commitment of a school's professional staff. There is no more critical function for school leaders than ensuring that staff members dedicated to continuous improvement are recruited, recognized, rewarded, and retained. High turnover and the constant replacement of large numbers of staff members undermine efforts to sustain school success.

KEY LESSONS AND NEXT STEPS

Several key lessons are associated with successful efforts by leaders like Mel Riddile to sustain early improvements in school performance. Among these lessons are the following:

- Sustaining school success requires addressing the needs of high achievers as well as struggling students.
- The strongest teachers should provide instruction for the weakest students.
- Sustained success requires moving beyond a focus on getting students to pass standardized tests.
- Providing timely and targeted assistance to struggling students depends on teacher awareness, understanding, competence, commitment, and persistence.
- A continuum of interventions is needed to ensure that all students receive appropriate assistance.

To ensure that success continues to characterize the performance of an improving school, these steps may be necessary:

- The focus on intervention must be balanced by systematic efforts to prevent academic problems from developing in the first place.
- Efforts must be made to cultivate leadership within the faculty.
- Targets for school improvement should continue to be set on an annual or semiannual basis.
- Provisions for leader succession should be in place to ensure continuity of capable leadership.

PART IV

The Challenge of Creating a New School

The challenges presented in the preceding three sections all involved leading an existing school. To be sure, preventing school decline, turning around a low-performing school, and sustaining school improvement require school leaders to make significant changes in various aspects of school programs and operations, but these changes are of a different order of magnitude compared to designing a school from scratch. Chapter 7 draws on several examples of school leaders who created new schools in order to address specific problems that were not being addressed adequately in conventional school settings. In each case these leaders were guided by a philosophy or set of beliefs about how students learn and how they should be taught and treated.

7

Leadership for Students Who Need a Different Learning Environment

W hen Jay Strickler sized up the most important problems facing his Franklin County, Virginia, school division in the mid-1990s, he had no trouble pinpointing two. Strickler was a central office administrator at the time, but he would soon change his role and take the lead in designing and heading a new school. The first problem he saw involved Franklin County's rapid growth, thanks in large part to its proximity to fast-growing Roanoke, Virginia. The county needed a new high school and a new middle school, but resources were limited in the rural county. Per capita income for Franklin County in 1994 was less than $16,000, and 32 percent of students qualified for free or reduced-price meals. Two out of five adults lacked a high school diploma. The school division would be lucky to get sufficient funds to build a new middle school. A new high school was out of the question.

The second problem involved the large number of Franklin County students who opted to take non-college-preparatory courses in the eighth and ninth grades. These questionable decisions meant that many students were unprepared to consider college when they reached their junior and senior years. Strickler felt that much of Franklin County's high drop-out rate could be traced to the culture of low expectations that characterized the middle school. At 6 percent annually, the county's drop-out rate was one of the highest in the state.

Strickler and Superintendent Len Gereau believed that the key to reducing the drop-out rate and increasing the number of students leaving high school for college or at least relatively high-paying jobs involved the eighth grade. If they could take advantage of the need for a new middle school, then perhaps a new type of learning environment could be designed, one that would motivate eighth graders to tackle challenging coursework by exposing them to attractive career possibilities.

LEADING BY DESIGN

KEY QUESTIONS

1. What is the justification for designing a new school or learning environment?

2. What assumptions about teaching and learning need to be challenged?

3. What must be done to mobilize support for and implement a new school design?

Creating the Center for Applied Technology and Career Exploration

Jay Strickler and his colleagues needed to develop a new middle school for the students of rural Franklin County, Virginia. The one middle school serving the county was outdated and overcrowded. They could have opted to replace the facility with one that essentially functioned like its predecessor. They instead saw an opportunity to address some longstanding concerns in new and more effective ways.

Franklin County educators were aware that middle school was a source of academic problems. Eighth graders in particular exhibited little interest in tackling challenging subject matter or working on career-oriented goals. A variety of reasons might have accounted for these feelings: Lack of constructive role models. Uninspiring curriculum. Unsympathetic teachers. Overactive hormones. And so on. School leaders in Franklin County took a hard look at their eighth graders and determined that many of them struggled because they failed to see any connection between their schoolwork and life after school. Coming from a relatively poor county with little industry and few career opportunities, students had little idea of the vocational possibilities that were available. Strickler was convinced that students needed to be exposed to a variety of careers in an environment that allowed them to engage in the very activities that they might eventually undertake in the working world.

With the support of the superintendent and school board, Strickler formed eight teams, each devoted to a different career cluster. The clusters represented the following fields:

- Arts
- Natural resources and environmental protection
- Manufacturing
- Engineering and architectural design
- Media design
- Legal science
- Finance
- Health, medicine, and human services

Each career cluster encompassed jobs for which a college education was required as well as jobs for which a high school diploma was sufficient. Teams consisted of teachers, parents, and representatives from local businesses. Teams received input from a panel of experts in each of the particular career areas. Every team developed a set of core concepts to guide student work in the career cluster along with a general set of expectations for all eighth graders. These included the ability to do the following:

- Develop oral, written, and auditory communication skills
- Clarify a career path plan
- Develop a work ethic that includes responsibility, initiative, and dependability
- Solve problems effectively in diverse collaborative groups
- Apply problem-solving skills using appropriate technology
- Develop research skills using appropriate technology
- Develop strategies to adapt to change

After a year and a half of planning and team meetings, Strickler and his colleagues had a clear idea of what they wanted to accomplish. How to accomplish it was another matter altogether. At this point, adversity intruded and Franklin County school leaders were imaginative enough to turn it to their advantage. A bond referendum did not yield sufficient funds to build a middle school large enough to accommodate all of the county's middle school students. Rather than abandoning the considerable planning that had been done, Strickler entertained the possibility of building a facility that could accommodate half of the county's eighth graders and a smaller number of ninth graders, a total of roughly 500 students. There was no commandment etched in stone, he reasoned, that required all students to attend the same school all year. Why couldn't half of the eighth graders attend the new school for a semester and then switch places with the other half? Eighth graders, in other words, would spend a semester at the new school and a semester at the old middle school.

This unusual arrangement clearly would relieve the overcrowding problem, but it would also do something else. It enabled Franklin County to create an entirely unique learning environment. Strickler did not want the new facility to be anything like the old middle school, or any middle school for that matter. His vision was a facility that came as close as possible to a high-tech workplace for adults. Nothing about the facility should remind students that they were in school. Here was an opportunity to give young adolescents a real taste of the world after school. No bells. No classes. No gymnasium. No library. No lockers. No cafeteria.

Strickler, in his determination to create a "non-school," even insisted on a new vocabulary. Students should not be referred to as students; they were "interns." Teachers were "supervisors." Strickler, who had opted to leave his central office position in order to lead the new facility, became the "director," not the principal. And the new facility would be called the Center for Applied Technology and Career Exploration, or CATCE for short.

Strickler believed that the CATCE curriculum should be problem based. Students, in other words, would address the kinds of authentic problems that they might confront in an actual job. Problem-based learning, however, does not fit neatly into 45-minute periods. Students require longer blocks of time if they are to make any significant headway on solving a problem. Strickler wanted students to achieve the satisfaction of actually solving problems, not just taking a few preliminary steps. Furthermore, he and his colleagues felt that the kinds of problems to which students would be exposed mattered. They wanted students to work on problems to which the solutions would constitute a contribution to the community. Schools too often, they contended, ask students to achieve solely for their own benefit, not the benefit of others.

An example from the natural resources and environmental protection career cluster illustrates exactly what the CATCE planners hoped for. The two course supervisors (teachers) had students collect water samples from a local stream that was believed to be polluted. For several days, students wore old clothes to CATCE so they could go to the stream and collect the samples. They brought the samples back to CATCE and analyzed them, discovering in the process that the stream was indeed polluted. The remainder of their time in the natural resources and environmental protection "module" was spent preparing a proposal for the county water board on the steps needed to clean up the stream. The students then presented their proposal to the water board.

The students had six weeks to work on their problem. During each six-week module, students participate in only one career cluster. When they are preparing to attend CATCE, each eighth grader chooses three career cluster modules plus an alternate. The maximum number of students in a module is 30. They are supervised by two teachers, one of whom is a certificated teacher. In another unique feature of the CATCE design, the second teacher is an individual from the world of work. They might be a former forest ranger, legal assistant, or construction manager. Before these teachers could join their certificated teammates, Strickler had to obtain a waiver from the Virginia Department of Education. State officials gave their approval, recognizing that students can benefit from contact with individuals fresh from various occupations.

During each six-week module, students are assigned to small teams. Learning to cooperate on a team is an important goal of the CATCE experience. When teammates reach a stopping place in their work each day, they can go to lunch in the commons. There is no cafeteria period per se. Several food vendors from the community provide students with a variety of lunchtime options. The message Strickler wanted to convey is this: At CATCE, you will be treated as a responsible person and expected to behave accordingly.

The same approach applies to student attire. Students are expected to dress appropriately for the activities of the day. Jeans and sweatshirts might be fine for collecting stream samples, but presenting to the water board requires dresses for girls and coats and ties for boys.

When CATCE opened on August 25, 1997, there were approximately 800 eighth graders in Franklin County. Half of them attended CATCE in the fall and then went to the regular middle school while the other half came to CATCE for spring semester. Strickler made certain that CATCE's curriculum covered certain subjects required by the state's Standards of Learning. Other required subjects, such as social studies, were addressed at the middle school. Strickler planned to welcome back some ninth graders who wished to develop a concentration in one career cluster.

CATCE, to be sure, had its share of doubters. Some people in the community, for example, worried about how students would perform on state standardized tests. Others feared that students returning to the traditional middle school would be bored and become disruptive. No one was more pleased than Jay Strickler when the results came back for the 1999 state tests—the second year eighth graders took the new tests. Passing rate increases for Grade 8 English, mathematics, history, social studies, and science ranged from 14 to 21 percent. What's more, teachers in the traditional middle school made a concerted effort to enliven their courses and engage students. Design leadership by Jay Strickler had involved risks, but the risks had paid off. Eighth graders were excited about learning and making a contribution to their community.

Creating Central Park East Secondary School

New York City is a world away from rural Virginia, but Deborah Meier's leadership in designing Central Park East Secondary School (CPESS) reflects many of the qualities of Jay Strickler's leadership in developing CATCE. Both leaders wanted to address very real problems with the school experiences of students from disadvantaged backgrounds, and both were guided by strong beliefs about how students learn best and how they should be taught and treated. The challenge for each involved finding ways to convert good intentions and strong beliefs into smoothly functioning learning environments.

Meier cut her "design teeth" by creating Central Park East Elementary School (CPEES) in 1974. Her story is chronicled in *The Power of Their Ideas* (1995). Meier believed that a small school was preferable to a large one. A small school represented a learning environment in which teachers and students could build strong and productive relationships. Resources that might have gone to administration and supervision in a large school were freed for classroom use. She and her colleagues designed an environment in which student curiosity was encouraged and democracy was operationalized. Meier may have been the head of CPEES, but she maintained a full teaching load.

A decade after CPEES opened, Meier was ready to create a secondary school based on many of the principles that had guided the development of CPEES. She recognized the problems with which large, comprehensive secondary schools grappled. If "small" worked for elementary education, it also could work for middle and high school education. She believed that it was better to grow the new school than to start all grade levels simultaneously. In the fall of 1985, Central Park East Secondary School (CPESS) welcomed 80 seventh graders. Adding a grade level a year, CPESS eventually encompassed Grades 7 through 12 and enrolled 450 students.

Meier's leadership during the designing of CPESS was manifested in several important ways. First, she insisted on challenging assumptions about how teaching and learning should occur, what students should learn, and the settings in which they should learn. The result was a school design that made sense, not a design that fit a mold formed by tradition and state and district regulations.

Instead of structuring the school day around seven or eight relatively brief class periods, each devoted to a different subject matter area, Meier worked with her colleagues to develop two-hour interdisciplinary class periods. Rather than relying on short-answer tests to assess student progress, teachers required students to demonstrate learning by applying knowledge. Students engaged in developing "products" and presenting "exhibitions." Seminars, group work, tutorials, coaching, and independent study replaced traditional lectures and seat work. Because these changes required a much greater level of teacher involvement, class sizes were not allowed to exceed 20 students. Meier acknowledged that many design features of CPESS were influenced by the philosophy of John Dewey and the principles of Essential Schools (as articulated by Ted Sizer).

The process Meier followed in designing CPESS mirrored her commitment to democratic values. This value-based orientation constitutes the second important dimension of her leadership. Meier (1995) describes the design process as follows:

> Planning CPESS required us to articulate our own separate points of view in ways that our colleagues could understand, and then to hear and understand theirs. In the course of this sharing of views I think we built a stronger school. (p. 39)

When a bold new design for a school is created, it is tempting to think that it sprung full-blown from the head of a visionary school leader. The experience of planning CPESS serves as a reminder that design leadership also can entail facilitating productive dialogue among various stakeholders. Meier, to be sure, possessed strong beliefs about teaching and learning, but she held an even stronger belief in the value of stakeholder participation. Students, parents, and teachers all provided valuable input into the design process.

Meier's value-oriented leadership, like Jay Strickler's, was manifested in her belief that students should contribute to the communities in which they live. A key element of the CPESS program is the community service component that requires every student to spend a minimum of three hours each week out in the community providing service.

Community service was one way Meier believed that student responsibility could be cultivated. Another way that CPESS promotes student responsibility involves the development by every 11th and 12th grader of a Process Portfolio. Each student is expected to demonstrate his or her knowledge and mastery of skills in this portfolio before receiving a diploma. In this way, students take charge of monitoring their learning.

The emphasis on student responsibility does not mean that CPESS students are "cast adrift" when they complete 10th grade. Upon entering the Senior Institute (11th and 12th grades), every student is assigned a Graduation Committee comprised of a family member, a staff member, an adult chosen by the student, a classmate, and an advisor. The student and their Graduation Committee prepare a customized program of study designed to prepare the student for graduation and the world beyond. Meier recognized that a good education is a collective effort.

The third dimension of Meier's design leadership was her ability to think systemically. Thinking systemically requires attention to and appreciation of the connections between people and between design elements. Instead of focusing on the language arts curriculum and the social studies curriculum as separate entities, for example, Meier encouraged CPESS teachers to explore the links between the two subject matter areas. This approach carried over into all phases of CPESS operations. Students needed to be connected to their community. Parents needed to be connected to the school. Teachers needed to be connected to their students not only as instructors but also as advisors. Teachers also needed to be connected to each other through joint planning and communal learning. Even when she envisioned the mission of CPESS, Meier embraced the importance of systemic thinking. Refusing to treat educational equity and educational excellence as dichotomous, Meier insisted that the two aims were inextricably linked.

The efficacy of Meier's design leadership is apparent in CPESS's longevity. Though Meier moved on to new challenges, the school has continued to post impressive statistics for student graduation. CPESS is not characterized by the discipline and attendance problems found in many secondary schools. Perhaps the greatest testament to CPESS's founding mother, however, is the fact that students and teachers alike enjoy being a part of the school community.

The Need for New Learning Environments

The notion that one generic learning environment can address the needs and aspirations of all students equally well is noble, to be sure, but perhaps unrealistic. The history of education reflects continuing experimentation with new designs for schools. Often these new designs eventually influence practice in mainstream schools and lead to widespread improvements in teaching and learning.

Jay Strickler recognized the fact that replacing Franklin County's old middle school with a more up-to-date clone was unlikely to address some of the fundamental problems facing educators in Franklin County. Why, he wondered, was the drop-out rate so high? Why were eighth graders opting for unchallenging courses? Could a facility and a program be designed for eighth graders that actually would motivate middle schoolers to become more engaged in and excited about their schooling? Design leaders begin by asking such bold questions.

Deborah Meier also manifested a similar curiosity. She wondered whether the American high school, which had proved so resistant to change over the years, could be redesigned in a way that served the cause of educational equity as well as educational excellence. Like Jay Strickler, she was well aware of the high drop-out rate in her community. She understood that failure to earn a high school diploma often condemned young people to lives of modest incomes, limited possibilities, or worse.

New designs for schools and learning environments often result from the commitment of school leaders to help students whose educational needs are not being served well by conventional programs. Such was the impetus for the creation of the Center for Applied Technology and Career Exploration and for the Central Park East Secondary School. The proliferation of alternative schools for students who are unable or unwilling to benefit from standard educational practices is further evidence of the value for new designs.

One such alternative school is Southeastern Regional Alternative School (SRAS) in rural Fauquier County, Virginia. The opportunity to create SRAS arose when the state provided funds to establish alternative schools serving two or more school divisions. Melody Hackney jumped at the chance to create a learning environment that relied more on positive reinforcement, patience, and compassion than threats and punishment. Her vision included a low teacher-student ratio (1 to 10) that would enable teachers to build constructive relationships with their students and foster a sense of community. A day at SRAS begins with a schoolwide meeting where announcements, goals, complaints, and concerns are shared. Later in the day, students again meet as a group, this time to address problems that particular students are experiencing. A third schoolwide meeting closes the school day and serves as an opportunity to reflect on the day, acknowledge what went well, and plan for upcoming activities.

Understanding that the students who would be sent to SRAS were referred primarily for disruptive behavior and truancy, Hackney devoted considerable time to thinking about behavior management. Punitive measures obviously were of limited value. Such measures already would have been tried before students arrived at SRAS. Hackney operated on the assumption that young people need a reason to change their behavior and, ultimately, a reason to change their lives. The focus of teacher-student advisory sessions and schoolwide meetings at SRAS often involves discussions of these matters. When students periodically exhibit unacceptable behavior, they are sent to an isolated classroom to reflect on their behavior and compose an essay explaining how they can avoid inappropriate behavior in the future.

A unique feature of Hackney's design involves the process by which students return to their referring middle school or high school. Hackney insisted that SRAS employ a "transition specialist." This individual negotiates arrangements for each student's return. In some cases, the return is accomplished in stages, with the student spending part of the day at SRAS and part in the referring school. The transition specialist continues to maintain contact with students after they leave SRAS to make certain that they receive the support and encouragement they need to succeed.

Like Strickler and Meier, Hackney was unwilling to accept conventional approaches to school design. Her leadership involved exploring a wide range of possibilities, choosing policies and practices that showed promise for a challenging group of students and mobilizing central office and community support for her design.

New designs for schools and learning environments do not necessarily arise only in response to the problems experienced by specific groups of students. In certain cases, school leaders strive to design a school or learning environment that reflects a particular theory of learning, philosophy, or set of beliefs. Deborah Meier was guided to some extent by the principles of Essential Schools as articulated by Ted Sizer. Best Practices High

School in Chicago resulted from the desire of a group of education professors to design a small high school around research-based teaching practices (Daniels, Bizar, & Zemelman, 2001). Members of the teacher cooperative that launched the New Country School, a public charter school in Henderson, Minnesota, were determined to design a school based on teacher professionalism (Toch, 2003). Across the United States, there are schools that reflect the beliefs of Maria Montessori, the experiential education approach of Outward Bound, and the behavior modification strategies of B. F. Skinner. The one thing that these diverse learning environments have in common is the fact that they do not resemble conventional schools and classrooms. It is safe to say that they probably would never have gotten off the drawing board unless some individual or group of individuals was willing to exercise leadership by challenging assumptions about teaching and learning.

A Willingness to Challenge Assumptions

At the heart of the school design process is a desire to interrogate seemingly sacred assumptions about how teaching and learning are supposed to be done. In order to design a new school or redesign an existing school, school leaders must think about various "design elements." These elements include the purposes and goals of learning, the content of learning, when learning takes place, where learning takes place, how learners are organized and instructed, the conditions under which learning takes place, and the criteria and methods for determining what has been learned (Duke, 2004, p. 109). Each of these design elements, of course, is subject to a set of prevailing assumptions. School leaders who desire to create new and improved learning environments must be willing to question each set of assumptions. Failing to do so almost ensures that the new learning environment will look and function a lot like conventional learning environments.

Take the matter of educational purposes and goals. Jay Strickler saw no reason why a program for eighth graders could not be developed as a first line of defense against high school dropouts. Deborah Meier regarded the cultivation of curiosity as a goal just as worthy as mastering a body of factual knowledge. Melody Hackney refused to think of an alternative school simply as a place to banish uncooperative young people.

Prevailing assumptions about curriculum emphasize the importance of the academic disciplines. Students must get an annual dose of language arts, mathematics, social studies, and science, preferably in discrete courses and lessons. Deborah Meier believed, however, that students were more likely to understand the relationships among and between the disciplines if the curriculum stressed *interdisciplinarity*. Jay Strickler shared a similar belief but chose to demonstrate the integration of knowledge in the context of career clusters and problem-based learning. Each cluster at CATCE required students to draw on skills derived from various disciplines in order to solve authentic problems. Melody Hackney's vision of important subject matter extended beyond academic disciplines to include interpersonal relations and personal development.

Convention dictates that secondary schools should be organized around a number of separate and equal class periods, ranging from less than an hour to an hour and a half. All three of the school leaders spotlighted in this chapter challenged the traditional daily schedule of middle schools and high schools. Hackney made sure ample time was set aside daily for community building. Meier insisted that students spend at least three hours out in the community engaged in a service activity. When students were back at CPESS, they often engaged in learning experiences that required extended periods of time. Strickler's design for CATCE called for students to spend all day, every day for six weeks in the same career cluster module completing a meaningful project.

When most educators think of school, they think of a facility with double-loaded corridors, a cafeteria, a gymnasium, and a library. Jay Strickler challenged this notion in several ways. First, he saw no reason why eighth graders had to spend both semesters in the same facility. Second, he believed that one of those semesters should be spent in a setting designed more like a high-tech workplace than a typical school. While CPESS did not boast a particularly innovative physical design, Deborah Meier believed that the spaces in which students learn should not be limited to the school building. The entire city became a learning environment for CPESS students.

When it came to the organization and delivery of instruction, the design leaders in this chapter also were willing to challenge prevailing assumptions. At CPESS, upperclassmen entered the Senior Institute where they were assigned a Graduation Committee to oversee their learning activities and ensure that they completed their studies and received their diploma. At SRAS, students frequently transitioned back to their referring school in stages and under the watchful eye of a transition specialist. Students at CATCE undertook problem-based learning under the supervision of two instructors, one of whom had recent experience in a field represented in the career cluster.

The conditions under which learning is expected to take place are typically characterized by a heavy emphasis on rules and punishments, arrangements that require students to work mostly on their own, and an equal amount of learning time for every student. Melody Hackney purposefully sought a balance between rule-governed behavior and caring. Relationships, not rules, were the key in her design to overcoming the problems her students previously had experienced in middle and high school. She did not insist that students return to their referring school until they felt they were ready. Guided by a desire to promote cooperative behavior, Jay Strickler encouraged CATCE instructors to organize activities so that students worked in teams. He recognized that teamwork was a key to success in the working world.

The last design element concerns the assessment of learning. Many educators assume that students should be assessed on their *acquisition* of knowledge. This belief leads to tests that focus on factual knowledge. Strickler and Meier challenged this practice by stressing the *application* of knowledge as the best indicator of learning. Through projects, exhibitions, and portfolios, students at CATCE and CPESS actually demonstrated what they had learned. Students at SRAS were expected to demonstrate that they could conduct themselves responsibly before Melody Hackney approved their return to the referring school.

The willingness to challenge assumptions was clearly manifested in the design leadership exhibited by each of the three individuals in this chapter. This inclination to question accepted practices did not cease when CATCE, CPESS, and SRAS opened their doors, however. True to their credentials as design leaders, Strickler, Meier, and Hackney continued to explore new and better ways of doing things, in the process challenging their own original ideas. As a consequence, the schools they helped to design have continued to evolve, even after they moved on to new challenges.

The Mobilization of Support

It takes vision, imagination, and no small amount of guts to challenge assumptions about the way teaching and learning are supposed to be done, but interpersonal skills, organizational expertise, and political savvy are needed to win support for bold new designs for schools and learning environments.

Jay Strickler made certain that community members and teachers were involved in every phase of CATCE's design, development, and implementation. After securing the Franklin County Board of Supervisor's support for the funding of a new facility and the Board of Education's approval for the project, Strickler and his colleagues met with representatives of business and industry to identify career clusters that would be attractive to students and that would lead to post–high school employment or further education. Following the identification of eight career clusters, a Curriculum Development Team consisting of parents, teachers, and individuals from relevant businesses was formed for each career cluster. Each team specified the skills and attributes employers were seeking and the curriculum content that should be covered in order to develop them. The process took over a year, but by the time it had been completed, the members of the eight Curriculum Development Teams constituted a cheerleading squad for CATCE.

Having mapped out the curriculum and identified desired outcomes for each career cluster, Strickler started looking for instructors. The CATCE faculty, he believed, should have a year to get prepared for the new facility's opening. Teacher teams needed time to get to know each other, develop problem-based projects, and understand the philosophy behind CATCE. Strickler also needed the ramp-up period to allay the concerns of some parents and teachers. Parents who wanted their children to attend college feared that CATCE might be too vocationally oriented. Strickler assured them that every career cluster involved careers requiring a college education as well as jobs open to high school graduates. For their part, many teachers at the old middle school wondered how their classes could compete with the exciting new learning opportunities that would be available to students during the semester they spent at CATCE. Strickler suggested that they might want to work on making their classes more engaging and project based.

Melody Hackney faced her share of skeptics as well. They questioned her "soft" approach to dealing with students with a history of disruptive and uncooperative behavior. High school teachers believed that students who were placed at SRAS would fall so far behind their peers academically that they would never be able to come back to their referring school and pick up where they had left off. After considerable negotiating with high school administrators, Hackney worked out an arrangement that allowed some students to complete their high school studies at the alternative school and still receive a diploma from their referring high school. For students who returned to their referring high school to complete coursework, Hackney created the role of transition specialist to provide continuing guidance and support and make certain students did not fall back on the bad habits that had resulted in their coming to SRAS in the first place.

Deborah Meier had less of a sales job to do for CPESS because school system officials and parents already had seen the benefits of her approach to teaching and learning at Central Park East Elementary School. The key decision for Meier involved growing CPESS one grade at a time rather than trying to launch a six-grade-level secondary school at one time. This approach enabled her to gradually build a faculty capable of operating in a unique learning environment and socialize students to a new approach to schooling.

What can make design leadership so challenging and so different from the leadership needed to address other challenges is the fact that it typically begins long before a school actually opens. Leaders start by identifying unmet needs and convincing others that teaching and learning can be undertaken in new and more productive ways. By the time an innovative design has been converted into a fully functioning learning environment, design leaders may have been at work for months or even years.

MEETING THE CHALLENGE OF CREATING A NEW SCHOOL

There are two ways to approach the development of a new school. One way involves focusing on replacing a current facility with a newer and larger (or smaller) version of the original. This is what many principals are called on to do when an existing school is found to be outdated, unsafe, or over-crowded. The second way requires school leaders to consider whether a new design, encompassing educational programs as well as physical space, can be created to address the needs of students who are not benefitting from their current learning environment. The second approach constitutes design leadership and represents a challenge quite distinct from preventing school decline, turning around a low-performing school, and sustaining school improvements over time.

Design leaders first must develop a convincing justification for deviating from conventional practice and then come up with an appropriate design. In order to ensure that the design represents an improvement, design leaders must be willing to challenge prevailing assumptions about teaching and learning and to explore a wide range of alternatives. Developing a worthy new design, however, is not the end of the design leader's work. Then they must mobilize the resources and support necessary to bring the design to life. To do so requires interpersonal and political skills as well as the ability to organize people to do something that may not have been done before.

KEY LESSONS AND NEXT STEPS

Among the lessons learned from school leaders who succeed in developing bold new learning environments are the following:

- Developing truly new learning environments requires that prevailing assumptions about teaching and learning be challenged.
- An important element of designing a new learning environment involves rethinking how each day is organized.
- Good school design entails systemic thinking (i.e., a focus on the connections between design elements).
- New designs of learning environments are likely to be regarded by some individuals and groups as a threat.

While the steps following the creation of a new design are likely to vary with each situation, it is likely that every school leader who develops a new design will need to undertake these steps:

- Broad-based support for implementing the new design must be mobilized.
- The ultimate success of the new design depends on execution—the ability of educators to convert the design into actual practice. The individual responsible for the original design is likely to be the person best prepared to oversee this process.
- Developing a new learning environment is not an event but a process. This process will require continued adjustments and fine tuning.

PART V

Leadership Lessons

The message of this book is straightforward—school leaders succeed in various ways, depending on the circumstances they face. There is no generic form of school leadership that is guaranteed to fit every challenge equally well. By the same token, school leaders can fail in various ways, depending on the circumstances they face. Chapter 8 discusses some of the ways that school leaders can undermine their own effectiveness. The concluding chapter provides an opportunity to reflect on the significance of differentiating school leadership and its implications for the preparation and development of school leaders.

8

Why School Leaders Fail

The first seven chapters of this book examine how school leaders succeed when faced with four distinct types of challenges. School leaders, like other leaders, are not always successful, however. Why do school leaders fail? The short answer goes like this—school leaders fail because they do not recognize the fact that different challenges call for different leadership responses.

It is just as important to understand why and how school leaders fail as it is to understand why and how they succeed. Just as the leadership required to address different challenges is likely to vary, so too are the ways that school leaders undermine their effectiveness. The approach that works well under one set of circumstances may not work well in another situation. In this chapter, we shall consider some of the sources of leadership failure in schools.

School leaders, of course, may fail to address a challenge successfully for reasons beyond their control—lack of central office support, for example, or an unforeseen loss of key staff members. It is the unique burden of leaders, however, that even when they are not the cause of problems that arise during their watch, they are expected to take responsibility for these problems. When leaders blame others for problems, they risk being seen as not in control of their own organizations.

SELF-INFLICTED PROBLEMS

The focus of this chapter is the problems that school leaders actually create for themselves, problems that with proper training and sound judgment should be avoidable. These problems include failure to anticipate a potential challenge to school effectiveness, reliance on false necessity, misdiagnosis of problematic conditions, excessive prioritization, choice of the wrong focus, choice of the wrong solution for addressing a problem, groupthink, delegation dilemmas, and failure to follow up and follow through.

The point of this chapter is not to suggest that the world can be blessed with perfect leaders if they only attend to the warning signs. All leaders make mistakes. The biggest mistake of all, however, is failing to learn from mistakes. Perhaps by reflecting on the leader-generated problems discussed in the pages to follow, school leaders will be more inclined to recognize when they have acted inappropriately and therefore less likely to repeat the mistake.

Failure to Anticipate a Challenge

Some challenges are virtually impossible to predict. In other cases, however, failure to anticipate a challenge is the result of human error. A leader ignores the warning signs or minimizes the likelihood of a serious threat. The failure is all the greater when a disaster occurs, and leaders still fail to take heed. Any school leader who did not develop or dust off a crisis management plan following the Columbine High School shootings arguably was guilty of negligence. Leaders are expected to keep their ears to the ground, monitor rumors, and seek information from a variety of sources in an effort to be prepared for any contingency.

Schools leaders who are unable to prevent a decline in student achievement may fail to take local demographic changes seriously. Principals who see a steady increase in the enrollment of English language learners or disabled students and neglect to address these changes with the faculty, develop appropriate assistance programs, arrange for staff development training, and seek support from the central office and the community have no one to blame but themselves when performance starts to drop. The special needs of these students are well known, and proven practices exist for addressing them.

School leaders sometimes appear to be caught off guard when they encounter resistance to reforms. Such resistance, however, is entirely predictable, even when the reforms are well thought out and justifiable. Bridges (2004) has pointed out that change invariably gives rise to a sense of loss, even when conditions are deplorable and merit change. The status quo is familiar to people. Change represents the unknown. It forces people out of their comfort zone and into new territory where they are likely to get lost. Prudent leaders expect such a reaction to reforms, at least by some individuals, and they prepare accordingly. Other leaders, however, simply get angry and upset when people challenge change.

It is reasonably safe to assume that school leaders at some point will need to deal with personnel turnover, dysfunctional personnel, ineffective teacher teams, tight budgets, enrollment changes, concerned parents, and public criticism. Such matters are endemic to schools. It would be a serious mistake for school leaders to think that these issues can be avoided by some combination of good intentions and positive thinking.

Reliance on False Necessity

Relying on false necessity in some ways is the polar opposite of failing to anticipate challenges. While the latter problem is characterized by leaders who are oblivious to the potential consequences of new developments, the former represents a predilection by leaders to define every unexpected development as a crisis. Just because a school experiences an unexpected influx of English language learners, for example, is no reason for a principal to sound the alarm or cause staff members to panic. Effective leadership under such circumstances involves anticipating the needs of the newcomers and taking steps in a calm and professional manner to address the needs. No one is well served by frantic and hasty action.

When school leaders elevate every problem to the level of an emergency, they risk desensitizing the staff and the community. The parable of the shepherd who cried "wolf" too often is instructive in this regard. Some specialists in organizational change rightly stress the need to create a sense of urgency in order to mobilize support for important change. School leaders must be careful, though, to avoid making *every* change appear as if it is urgently needed.

Invoking a sense of urgency too often can have a variety of negative consequences. People, over time, may become inured to calls for urgent action and consequently fail to take seriously a genuine emergency. A principal who treats every drop in test scores as a crisis demanding immediate changes in programs and practices is likely to make some serious mistakes and exhaust teachers in the process. New programs and practices typically require time to be implemented correctly. Frequent changes can result in the scrapping of worthy interventions that simply need more time to be put in place.

School leaders who insist too often that an immediate response is necessitated also reduce the likelihood that legitimate concerns will be voiced. Stakeholder buy-in frequently is contingent on the ability of individuals to express their doubts and misgivings. Silencing debate for the sake of expediency rarely contributes to the mobilization of support for action. It also may cause leaders to overlook or minimize ethical considerations and the possible long-term consequences of their actions.

It is tempting to equate leadership with decisiveness in the face of crisis. There are, of course, genuine emergencies when school leaders cannot afford to delay. When, however, such decisiveness precludes a careful examination of possible courses of action and their likely consequences and reduces the likelihood of mobilizing support, leaders are well advised to pause for a moment and consider the risks of premature action.

Misdiagnosis of Problems

It goes without saying that failure to identify the real cause of a problem greatly reduces the likelihood of choosing the correct solution. The medical profession is well aware of the harm that can result when physicians incorrectly diagnose patients' problems. So too are the lawyers who make a living off of malpractice suits. Concern over the potential for misdiagnosis leads to recommendations that patients solicit second opinions. Programs that prepare physicians emphasize the importance of "bedside manner" for good reason. When physicians are able to gain the trust of patients and put them at ease, they are more likely to obtain an accurate picture of the patients' condition.

School leaders, like physicians, are capable of misdiagnosis. A principal charged with turning around a low-performing school may decide that the source of the problem is inadequate parental involvement. The actual cause, however, may have more to do with the fact that students are not being taught the material they need to know in order to pass state tests. Another principal who is asked to develop an alternative school may determine that the facility is needed because some students suffer from behavior disorders. It turns out, though, that the students become frustrated in regular classes because they cannot read well.

Various factors can contribute to misdiagnosis of school problems. School leaders may jump to erroneous conclusions based on limited information. Principals often are told what staff members think they want to hear. Getting open and honest feedback about school conditions requires tapping multiple sources of information and identifying individuals who can be trusted to provide accurate information. A principal who wants to understand why ninth graders are getting low grades needs to talk with teachers, but he also must engage students and their parents in discussions of academic problems.

Sometimes, school leaders are only prepared to acknowledge certain causes of problems. People are products of their training and experience. A principal who has been trained as a guidance counselor may tend to trace problems to psychosocial dynamics. Another principal with experience coaching football may attribute school problems to a lack of teamwork. Engaging a number of individuals with different training and experience in the task of identifying the causes of school problems reduces the likelihood of misdiagnosis.

Yet another reason why school problems may be misdiagnosed involves failure to understand contextual matters. Every school exists in a community with its own unique characteristics and culture. Schools, other than new schools, have a history. Neglecting a school's history and community context can lead to serious errors in judgment. Consider the newly appointed principal of a rural high school. Fresh from a stint as assistant principal in an urban high school, she registers alarm when teachers complain that some students are falling asleep in class. Based on her previous experience, she suspects that the students may be using drugs. What she fails to realize is that the students who are falling asleep come from farms where they must awaken before sunrise to do chores!

Excessive Prioritization

The central argument of this book is that the ability of school leaders to deal effectively with different challenges is a function of focus. There is always more for educators to do than time available to do it. That is the nature of schooling. Every lesson can be refined and improved. Every student can benefit from more one-on-one assistance. All parents would appreciate a regular update on their child's progress. Every teacher could use additional professional development. Each day, however, is limited to 24 hours, and no educator can or should work all the time. The only answer is to develop priorities.

As we have seen in the preceding chapters, each challenge is associated with a somewhat distinct set of priorities. Leaders are expected to provide the direction needed to accomplish the mission. This is true regardless of whether the mission is to prevent a school from declining, turn around a low-performing school, sustain school improvement, or develop an innovative school from scratch. Providing direction, in operational terms, means distinguishing between objectives that *must* be accomplished and objectives that are desirable but that can be deferred. Given the fact that school leaders operate in a world of limited time and resources, they must establish priorities.

School leaders can run into trouble when they elevate every objective to a high priority. If everything is a high priority, nothing is a high priority. Staff members become confused about what to do first and where to concentrate their energies. Such confusion can cause individuals to move in different directions rather than pulling together in the same direction.

Choosing the Wrong Focus

Just because a school leader is able to develop a set of priorities is no guarantee of success. The possibility always exists that the wrong priorities may have been chosen. This was precisely the problem encountered by Paul Cunneen in Gerald Grant's (1988) account of troubles at Hamilton High School. Faced with Hamilton High's desegregation in the early

1970s, growing student unrest and misconduct, and mounting teacher frustration, Cunneen decided that a concerted effort was needed to eliminate tracking and offer coursework that was more relevant to the lives of students. He increased the number of elective courses and reassigned students who had been in basic courses to regular courses. Conditions at Hamilton High subsequently went from bad to worse. Academic performance plummeted, teachers abrogated their professional responsibilities in a show of sympathy for students, and behavior problems escalated, at times pushing the school to the brink of chaos.

Cunneen eventually was removed in 1977, and Joseph Kielecki was appointed principal. Kielecki chose to focus on a set of issues that differed from his predecessor's. To address rampant misconduct, he restored a uniform code of discipline, one that treated black and white students alike. He backed up teachers in their efforts to regain control of classrooms and corridors. To re-establish academic integrity, he cut back on the number of electives, many of which had contributed little to students' intellectual growth. Within several years, Hamilton High once again was regarded as a good high school.

When a school has been low performing for some time, the source of the problem often involves deficiencies in students' ability to read and write. To choose a focus other than literacy improvement would be questionable under the circumstances. If academic challenges are accompanied by high levels of discipline problems, then it only makes sense also to focus on restoring order. There is a "chicken and egg" quality to focusing on discipline, however. School leaders must make a judgment regarding the origins of discipline problems. If discipline problems derive from poor instruction, it first may be necessary to zero in on instructional improvement. The better the initial diagnosis of problematic conditions, the more likely school leaders will select the appropriate focus.

Choosing the Wrong Solution

School leaders may correctly identify a focus and still encounter problems because they fail to select a good strategy for addressing the focal area of concern. Imagine that a principal rightly determines that literacy should be the focus for her faculty. She decides that all teachers should double the amount of time devoted to literacy instruction. If teachers lack the skills to teach literacy effectively or if the school's reading program is outdated and ineffective, doubling the time devoted to literacy instruction may only exacerbate the problem.

The likelihood of choosing a program, practice, or policy that fails to address a need is increased dramatically when school leaders only consider one or two options. How many times has a principal returned from a conference absolutely convinced that the new program that was presented at the conference is the right program for his school? Instead of a thorough search of available options, the principal asks his faculty to decide between the current program and the new program. Such a course of action is very risky.

School leaders may feel pressured to make a quick decision about a reform. They consequently do not take time to examine various alternatives. Slavin (1998) offers the following comment in this regard:

> One general problem of innovation is that school staffs choose a model of reform because it happens to be available at the point when a school is ready and able to make a change. Rarely do schools make considered choices among a set of attractive options to find a match between the model's characteristics and the school's needs and capabilities. (p. 1309)

It is the responsibility of school leaders to insist on reviewing all or most of the available alternatives before deciding on a particular reform. Instead of rushing to judgment and running the risk of making an incorrect choice, school leaders should seek out as much information as possible on reform options. This includes relevant research and field-based evaluation data. The program that Jay Strickler and his colleagues developed for CATCE took over two years to plan and entailed consideration of dozens of possibilities, but in the end, they had a unique learning environment that successfully addressed the needs of their students.

Choosing the wrong reform can have a number of negative consequences. First and foremost, the needs of students are not well served. If the reform is chosen to address deficits in their learning, its failure can jeopardize their chances of advancing. Second, precious time, energy, and resources are wasted when an incorrect choice is made. Finally, the chances of mobilizing support for future reforms are reduced. Teachers in particular become resistant to change when they must invest their time and energy in ill-chosen innovations.

Groupthink

Contemporary principals frequently rely on some form of leadership team to assist them in planning, decision making, and problem solving. Teams typically include assistant principals, representatives from special education and guidance, and teacher leaders (representing grade levels and academic areas). Some leadership teams function as highly effective groups, providing a range of perspectives and offering wise counsel to principals. In other cases, however, leadership teams are characterized by groupthink.

According to Janis (1972), groupthink represents the dynamics of groups in which the members are less concerned about making good decisions than they are in maintaining their own self-esteem vis-à-vis other group members. They also are especially deferential toward the leader of the group. Instead of questioning the leader's positions and raising possible problems with the leader's preferences, group members fall into line behind whatever course of action (or inaction) is favored by the leader. Such "rubber-stamping" may please the leader, but it does little to prevent bad decisions from being made. It is up to school leaders to see that groupthink is avoided.

In order to avoid groupthink, a school leader first has to recognize when it is present. Janis (1972) identified various warning signs. When group members get along famously and devote considerable energy to deflecting criticism of the leader's actions, groupthink may be at work. Other signs include the presumption that silence in meetings implies support and a preference for consensus rather than voting.

In order to avoid groupthink, school leaders should keep their preferences to themselves until they have listened to all team members. They need to encourage doubts, even to the point of assigning a group member to play the role of devil's advocate. Regardless of the challenges facing school leaders, they cannot overcome them alone. Teamwork is essential. The research on groupthink, however, serves as a warning that teamwork can be done poorly as well as productively.

Delegation Dilemmas

School leaders, especially very talented ones, can undermine their effectiveness by failing to delegate authority. Initially, of course, a principal who takes over a low-performing school may need time to determine which staff members are capable of handling additional responsibilities. As soon as possible, however, the principal must enlist the help of selected individuals. The problem with some very talented leaders is that they believe no one can do a particular task as well as they can. This may be true for a single task, but principals never are faced with only one task at a time. Eventually, trying to oversee every task will catch up with most leaders. The result is likely to be fatigue and less-than-ideal performance. Failure to delegate important responsibilities also sends a negative message to staff members: They cannot be trusted to handle key duties.

In certain cases, of course, individual staff members actually should not be entrusted with important responsibilities. Assigning such vital tasks as coordinating curriculum alignment and arranging staff development training to individuals who lack the competence and leadership to follow through can be just as harmful as failing to delegate at all. The ability to judge which staff members are likely to handle delegated responsibilities effectively is one of the greatest assets a principal can possess.

Success in selecting capable staff members to whom to delegate responsibilities, however, is not without its own risks. The staff of a school can become polarized when a principal is perceived to exhibit favoritism

... to certain individuals. Principals obviously ... when it comes to distributing leadership. While there is ... completely free of risk, principals who avoid ... find ways to learn about every individual ... accomplish, and how they are regarded by ...

... ollow Through

... many times: School leaders are busy people. ... al should be able to give clear instructions ... mplished and rest assured that the instruc- ... ly. Though the world is far from ideal, some ... e. They seem surprised when they discover that staff members failed to follow instructions.

Effective school leaders understand that they must follow up to ensure that their directions have been understood and carried out. Teachers are busy professionals, just as principals are. They must juggle a variety of responsibilities. It is not unusual under such circumstances to find that certain tasks are neglected or undertaken in a cursory manner. In other cases, the original instructions or expectations were communicated unclearly. When principals convey directions without checking to see that they have been understood, they have no one to blame but themselves if things do not turn out as hoped.

Failing to follow up is one kind of self-inflicted problem; failing to follow through is quite another. To follow through is to do what one said one would do. When a principal tells a teacher that she will notify her regarding the disposition of a disciplinary referral, she risks losing the teacher's trust when she fails to do so. When a principal asks teachers to share their concerns and then does nothing to address them, he is laying the groundwork for dissatisfaction. Effective school leadership depends on stakeholders being able to count on leaders to deliver on their promises.

THE GREATEST MISTAKE OF ALL

This book has focused on the ways effective school leadership varies with particular challenges. Just as there is not one way to lead, there is not one way that leaders fail. There is relatively little systematic research on the problems that school leaders create for themselves and their schools. It is unclear, for instance, whether certain types of mistakes are more likely to be made when leaders deal with certain types of challenges. It may be, for example, that excessive prioritization is more apt to occur when a principal tries to turn around a low-performing school than when she or he designs a new school.

There are enough problems to address in leading a school without school leaders making avoidable mistakes. Still, principals and other school leaders are human, and from time to time, mistakes probably are inevitable. The greatest mistake of all is failing to learn from one's mistakes. Mistakes function like compound interest. They build on each other over time. When school leaders do not learn lessons from the mistakes they make, they increase the likelihood that additional mistakes will be made.

9

The Implications of Differentiating Leadership

Golfers tell a joke about a gorilla that learned to play golf. Blessed with amazing strength and balance, the gorilla could drive a golf ball over 400 yards. Two golfers intent on winning a tournament decided to invite the gorilla and its owner to make up a foursome. When the gorilla got to the first tee, he drove the green, a distance of 415 yards. The ball landed just about a foot from the hole. The gorilla's playing partners were ecstatic. They began to think about how they would spend the prize money. When they reached the green, one of the players said to the gorilla's owner, "That gorilla can really drive a golf ball. How does he putt?" The owner replied, "Just like he drives!"

A golfer that drives the ball 400 yards and also putts the ball 400 yards is a dubious asset. Good putting demands a different set of skills than good driving. The joke illustrates the main point of this book. Leaders who address every challenge in the same way are unlikely to be very effective.

History is full of examples that confirm this position. Winston Churchill, for instance, was a great wartime leader, but he struggled in his efforts to lead Great Britain following World War II. The challenges were different. Mobilizing resources to combat a terrifying enemy is one thing; reviving a devastated economy is quite another.

When we step back and consider school leadership in general, it is tempting to think about the responsibilities that all principals share. These are the responsibilities covered in most preservice training programs: budgeting, teacher supervision and evaluation, school safety, planning, and so on.

When we take a few steps closer and zero in on particular school situations, though, it becomes clear that there is more to school leadership than a set of generic skills. There are qualitative differences between such challenges as preventing school decline, turning around a chronically low-performing school, sustaining school improvements over time, and creating an innovative new school. It may be true that all leaders need to set priorities, but the nature of those priorities varies with the circumstances. Setting the wrong priorities for the situation can be just as disastrous as failing to set any priorities or, conversely, deciding that everything is a priority.

The world of the school leader is a world of trade-offs. School leaders must be able to project into the future and assess the likely consequences of attending to one pressing concern versus competing concerns. Effective leadership is as much a function of knowing what not to do as it is a function of knowing what to do.

The value of differentiating school leadership is contained in a single word—*focus*. Knowing what to focus on when faced with a particular challenge can spell the difference between success and failure. Table 9.1

Table 9.1   Different Challenges, Different Priorities

Preventing school decline	Determine needs of new students Assess school's capacity to meet needs
Turning around a low-performing school	Focus on literacy, math, and discipline Achieve "quick wins" to boost confidence Cultivate teacher teams
Sustaining school improvements	Strengthen curriculum beyond literacy and math Develop a continuum of interventions Work on school reculturing
Designing an innovative school	Challenge assumptions about learning and teaching Examine a wide range of program options Mobilize broad-based support

reviews the four challenges described in this book and what actual school leaders focused on in order to address them.

Realizing that the number of Hispanic students attending Waverly Elementary School was growing, Eli Buck understood the importance of determining their educational needs and the capacity of his faculty to attend to them. Having determined that language acquisition was the greatest need of Waverly's newcomers, Buck arranged for professional development for teachers and the reassignment of teachers. Classes designed to accommodate different levels of language proficiency had to be added. Most importantly, teacher beliefs about the capabilities of new students needed to be addressed and adjusted.

Wilma Williams realized that Keswick Elementary School could not be turned around in a short amount of time unless teachers concentrated on improving instruction in reading. To facilitate this effort, she adjusted the school schedule to provide more time for literacy instruction and remediation. She also insisted that literacy instruction was the responsibility of all staff members. By achieving a few "quick wins" and promoting a team-based approach to literacy instruction, she was able to raise student achievement in a short period of time.

Mel Riddile also managed to turn around his school, but in order to sustain his initial success at Stuart High School, he needed to change his focus. To be a top-performing high school, the entire curriculum, not just English and mathematics, needed to be upgraded. Instead of one or two sources of assistance for struggling students, Stuart required a continuum of interventions covering everything from the identification of incoming at-risk ninth graders to credit recovery opportunities for upperclassmen. Another key to sustained success at Stuart was the development of a new school culture, one based on a belief in collaboration, continuous improvement, and high expectations.

The leadership exhibited by Jay Strickler, Deborah Meier, and Melody Hackney was directed at creating new and innovative learning environments. Each leader needed to challenge conventional beliefs about learning and teaching and explore a wide range of possibilities. Once new designs had been developed, they had to mobilize sufficient support to move from the drawing board to reality.

The intention behind *Differentiating School Leadership* is not to suggest that Eli Buck, Wilma Williams, Mel Riddile, Jay Strickler, Deborah Meier, and Melody Hackney neglected such managerial duties as building a sound budget and seeing that supplies were ordered. All school leaders must see that a variety of commonplace functions are completed in order for schools to operate smoothly. What distinguishes them, however, is not their routine managerial competence but their extraordinary capacity to focus energy and resources in ways that addressed the particular challenges confronting their schools.

SOME PRACTICAL CONSEQUENCES

The time has come to raise the "So what?" question. If we acknowledge that school leaders face a variety of challenges and that one generic approach to leadership is unlikely to work for every challenge, what are the practical implications of such a position? In this section, implications for the preparation, selection, evaluation, and study of school leaders will be discussed.

School Leader Preparation

Most preservice programs for preparing school leaders are based on a sequence of courses dictated, to some extent, by state credentialing standards. The standards tend to be similar from state to state. They cover aspects of school law and finance, teacher supervision and evaluation, general principles of administration, and school and community relations. In an effort to keep up with the demands of educational accountability, many programs have added content on data-based decision making and instructional leadership. The message is clear—all prospective principals need to know a common core of information and be able to undertake a common set of functions in order to secure an administrative credential and begin practice.

Recognition that generic leader preparation may not be sufficient for all schools and circumstances is limited to a small number of programs that claim to focus on urban school leadership or rural school leadership. It is interesting to note that, despite the vast number of suburban schools, there are no preparation programs devoted exclusively to their leadership.

In recent years, some states have begun to differentiate between the initial credential for principals and an advanced credential. Virginia, for example, requires administrators to work for five years before seeking the advanced credential. This credential can be earned in several ways, including completing a doctoral degree program and successfully undertaking a school improvement project. The introduction of an advanced credential is a signal that school leaders are not "finished products" when they complete their preservice coursework.

If a novice administrator has always worked in the same school or the same type of school, he or she may be unaware of the impact that different challenges can have on school leaders. To properly prepare prospective principals, preservice programs should expose students to a variety of challenges that they eventually might face and underscore the importance of differentiating leadership. Coursework should include case studies illustrating these different challenges, work on organizational diagnostics and the way school leaders can undermine their own effectiveness, and provide opportunities to practice determining priorities, given various sets of circumstances.

Preservice exposure to the need for differentiating school leadership is unlikely, of course, to provide all the preparation needed to deal with the prospect of school decline, to turn around a failing school, to sustain school improvement, or to design an innovative new school. But it is a beginning, and it alerts fledgling administrators to the limitations of a generic view of school leadership. Once individuals have begun to gain some initial experience as assistant administrators, the timing may be better to provide programs that focus on leadership for particular challenges. Advanced credentials might encompass training to address a variety of challenges or training that specializes in leading certain types of schools.

Highly focused training for school turnaround specialists has begun to be offered by a number of states. Virginia was the first state to launch such a program in 2004. Then Governor Mark Warner had seen turnaround specialists succeed in the private sector, and he felt a similar type of leadership could work in chronically low-performing schools. The result was the creation at the University of Virginia of the Darden-Curry Partnership for Leaders in Education, a collaboration between the Darden Graduate School of Business Administration, the Curry School of Education, and the Virginia Department of Education. The multi-year training program involves veteran principals who have been assigned to turn around low-performing schools. They receive advanced instruction in business principles and education best practices, all oriented to helping achieve dramatic improvements in a short period of time. The curriculum includes data and project management, how to create highly effective teams, and instructional interventions for struggling students.

Programs like the University of Virginia's illustrate the fact that the challenges facing today's school leaders are sufficiently different to warrant highly specialized training, training that extends far beyond what is received in most preservice preparation programs. Given the needs of chronically low-performing schools, principals charged with turning them around may need advanced training in how to select an appropriate reading program, how to evaluate the mathematics and special education curriculums, the effectiveness of different types of instructional interventions, threat assessment and school safety, and strategies for securing additional resources. Principals confronting other challenges are likely to benefit from other forms of highly specialized training.

School Leader Selection and Evaluation

The recognition that different challenges require different responses from school leaders has implications for how they are selected and evaluated. Ideally, of course, superintendents would be able to choose principals who already had success facing the same kinds of challenges presently confronting the schools in need of new leadership. The demand for principals with a track record of success meeting various challenges, unfortunately, exceeds the supply. Superintendents frequently must make selections from the ranks of the untested. Under such circumstances, superintendents can use the information on differentiating school leadership to pinpoint the necessary priorities for a particular school and then identify candidates who have the knowledge and skills to address these priorities.

If a superintendent is searching for a school leader to turn around a chronically low-performing school, for example, and she or he cannot find a candidate with a track record of success, it makes sense to search for someone who understands how to address the improvement of instruction in literacy. If a school faces an influx of English language learners, familiarity with the needs and culture of the newcomers would be desirable. When a superintendent is able to anticipate specialized school leadership needs well in advance, an effort also can be made to recruit promising individuals from the ranks of teachers and other professional staff. The school system then can arrange for these recruits to earn an administrative credential and receive the added training needed to prepare them for particular challenges.

If a superintendent has no luck finding an appropriate principal, another alternative course of action involves developing a school leadership team with the collective expertise required to address a particular challenge. There clearly are benefits to engaging the talents of reading specialists, special education directors, guidance counselors, and department chairs in providing school leadership. The key to their success, however, will depend on their ability to set aside parochial preferences and consider the overall needs of the school.

A third alternative involves finding a retired principal with experience addressing a particular challenge who is willing to work in tandem with a principal for a limited period of time. Such on-the-job mentoring and support has proven to be helpful in several states that assign veteran "coaches" to work with principals of low-performing schools.

When school leaders are enlisted to tackle a particular challenge, their evaluation should be tied to how well they undertake the task at hand. To underscore the importance of focus in differentiating school leadership, the evaluation of school leaders should be similarly focused. The expectations for a principal charged with sustaining a school improvement initiative should not be identical to those for a principal assigned the task of designing and opening a new school. Priorities vary depending on the challenges facing a school, and evaluations, to be effective, should reflect these varying priorities.

Research on School Leadership

Research on school leadership until the late 1970s reflected the same orientation as the preparation of school leaders. The focus was on generic school leadership and the common attributes of effective school leaders. Few efforts were made to distinguish leader effectiveness under different circumstances. The research on school effectiveness that began in the late 1970s zeroed in on principals who had managed to improve student achievement in low-performing, primarily urban elementary schools. By the beginning of the 21st century, researchers had gained substantial knowledge of what leaders needed to do to turn around low-performing schools, and they were beginning to investigate successful leadership associated with other challenges.

Based on the benefits of differentiating school leadership, three research-related recommendations are in order. First, researchers need to continue to study what successful school leaders do to prevent school decline in the face of demographic and financial challenges, to sustain school improvements over time, and to create innovative learning environments. The knowledge base regarding how to turn around low-performing high schools also can be expanded.

A second important focus for research concerns the *failure* of school leaders to meet the challenges discussed in this book. There are virtually no systematic studies of unsuccessful school leaders. Without such research, it is impossible to determine whether certain kinds of mistakes are more likely to be made when school leaders address certain kinds of challenges. Individuals involved in preparing school leaders need to know where principals go wrong. Do they, for example, fail to address a particular challenge successfully because of deficient skills in specific areas, errors in judgment, character flaws, factors beyond their control, or other reasons?

A third important focus for research concerns the ability of school leaders to adjust their leadership in the face of new and different challenges. To what extent can a principal who has designed and implemented a new school, for instance, go on to deal successfully with a threat to the school's academic success? Mel Riddile was able to turn around Stuart High School and then provide the leadership necessary to sustain and expand on early success. Is it possible to train others to do so? Researchers need to study school leaders as they move from one challenge to another.

LAST WORD

All schools need leadership. This is not the issue. The issue is this—Do all schools need the same kind of leadership? The position taken in this book is that school leaders face a variety of challenges, and these challenges can be so different that they require qualitatively different leadership responses. The verdict is still out as to whether particular individuals can make the adjustments necessary to address various challenges. It is important, however, for those charged with preparing, selecting, evaluating, and studying school leaders to recognize the importance of differentiating school leadership.

References

Allington, R. L. (2006). *What really matters for struggling readers* (2nd ed.). Boston: Pearson.

Arias, M. B., Faltis, C., & Cohen, J. (2007). Issues of cultural pluralism, successful school settings, and integrated relations. In E. Frankenburg & G. Orfield (eds.), *Lessons in Integration.* Charlottesville, VA: University of Virginia Press, 101–112.

Barone, M. (2002, February 8). Debating bilingual education. *U.S. News and World Report.* Retrieved January 22, 2009, from http://www.usnews.com/usnews/opinion/baroneweb/mb_020208.htm

Bingham, C. S., Harman, P., & Embree, H. (1997). *Scheduling for grade team planning in the elementary school: A formative evaluation.* Paper presented at the Annual Meeting of the North Carolina Association for Research in Education.

Blankstein, A. M. (2004). *Failure is not an option.* Thousand Oaks, CA: Corwin.

Bridges, W. (2004). *Transitions* (2nd ed.). Cambridge, MA: DaCapo Press.

Britz, J. (2007). *The first 90 days of the new middle school principal in a turnaround school: A case study.* Unpublished doctoral dissertation, Rossier School of Education, University of Southern California.

Canady, R. L., & Rettig, M. D. (2008). *Elementary school scheduling.* Larchmont, NY: Eye on Education.

Cech, S. J. (2008, July 30). Building bridges to the future. *Education Week, 27*(37), 22–24.

Chenoweth, K. (2007). *It's being done.* Cambridge, MA: Harvard Education Press.

Clark, R. M. (1983). *Family life and school achievement.* Chicago: University of Chicago Press.

Comer, J. P. (2004). *Leave no child behind.* New Haven: Yale.

Dana Center. (2002). *Expecting success: A study of five high performing, high poverty schools.* The Dana Center at the University of Texas and the Council of Chief State School Officers.

Daniels, H., Bizar, M., & Zemelman, S. (2001). *Rethinking high school.* Portsmouth, NH: Heinemann.

Darling-Hammond, L. (1997). *The right to learn.* San Francisco: Jossey-Bass.

Deal, T. E., & Peterson, K. D. (1999). *Shaping school culture.* San Francisco: Jossey-Bass.

Diamond, J. (2005). *Collapse.* New York: Viking.

Duke, D. L. (1987). *School leadership and instructional improvement.* New York: Random House.

Duke, D. L. (2002). *Creating safe schools for all children.* Boston: Allyn & Bacon.

Duke, D. L. (2004). *The challenges of educational change.* Boston: Pearson.

Duke, D. L. (2005). *Education empire: The evolution of an excellent suburban school system.* Albany, NY: State University of New York Press.

Duke, D. L. (2006). Keys to sustaining successful school turnarounds. *ERS Spectrum, 24*(4), 21–35.

Duke, D. L. (2008a). *The little school system that could: Transforming an urban school system.* Albany, NY: State University of New York Press.

Duke, D. L. (2008b). Understanding school decline. *International Studies in Educational Administration, 36*(2), 46–65.

Duke, D. L., Grogan, M., & Tucker, P. D. (2003). Educational leadership in an age of accountability. In D. L. Duke, M. Grogan, P. D. Tucker, & W. Heinecke (eds.), *Educational leadership in an age of accountability.* Albany, NY: State University of New York Press, 198–213.

Duke, D. L., & Meckel, A. M. (1980). The slow death of a public high school. *Phi Delta Kappan, 61*(10), 674–677.

Duke, D. L., Tucker, P. D., Belcher, M., Crews, D., Harrison-Coleman, J., et al. (2005). *Lift-off: Launching the school turnaround process in ten Virginia schools.* Charlottesville, VA: Darden-Curry Partnership for Leaders in Education, University of Virginia.

Duke, D. L., Tucker, P. D., Salmonowicz, M. J., & Levy, M. (2007). How comparable are the perceived challenges facing principals of low-performing schools? *International Studies in Educational Administration, 35*(1), 3–21.

Duke, D. L., Tucker, P. D., Salmonowicz, M. J., & Levy, M. (2008). U-turn required: How Virginia's first school turnaround specialists are meeting the challenges of improving low-performing schools. In W. Hoy & M. DiPaola (eds.), *Improving schools: Studies in leadership and culture.* Charlotte, NC: Information Age Publishing, 137–167.

Elmore, R. F. (2007). *School reform from the inside out.* Cambridge, MA: Harvard Education Press.

Evans-Stout, K. (1998). Implications for collaborative instructional practice. In D.G. Pounder (ed.), *Restructuring schools for collaboration.* Albany, NY: State University of New York Press, 121–134.

Fiedler, F. E. (1964). A contingency model of leadership effectiveness. In L. Berkowitz (ed.), *Advances in Experimental Social Psychology, 1.* New York: Academic Press, 149–190.

Fiedler, F. E. (1967). *A theory of leadership effectiveness.* New York: McGraw-Hill.

Flanagan, A., & Grissmer, D. (2005). The role of federal resources in closing the achievement gap. In J. E. Chubb & T. Loveless (eds.), *Bridging the achievement gap.* Washington, DC: Brookings.

Frankenberg, E. (2007). School integration—the time is now. In E. Frankenberg & G. Orfield (eds.), *Lessons in integration.* Charlottesville, VA: University of Virginia Press, 7–27.

Frazier, P., & Salmonowicz, M. J. (2006). *Pleasant Valley Elementary School: Celebrating success one student at a time.* Charlottesville, VA: Darden Graduate School of Business Administration, University of Virginia.

Fullan, M. (2001). *Leading in a culture of change.* San Francisco: Jossey-Bass.

Gardiner, M. E., & Enomoto, E. K. (2006). Urban school principals and their role as multicultural leaders. *Urban Education, 41*(6), 560–584.

Goleman, D., Boyatzis, R., & McKee, A. (2002). *Primal leadership: Realizing the power of emotional intelligence.* Boston: Harvard Business School Press.

Grant, G. (1988). *The world we created at Hamilton High.* Cambridge, MA: Harvard University Press.

Hargreaves, A., & Fink, D. (2006). *Sustainable leadership.* San Francisco: Jossey-Bass.

Hawley, W. D. (2007). Designing schools that use student diversity to enhance learning of all students. In E. Frankenberg & G. Orfield (eds.), *Lessons in integration.* Charlottesville, VA: University of Virginia Press, 31–56.

Herman, R., Dawson, P., Dee, T., Greene, J., Maynard, R., & Redding, S. (2008). *Turning around chronically low-performing schools.* Washington, DC: U.S. Department of Education, Institute for Education Sciences.

Hersey, P., & Blanchard, K. H. (1969). Life-cycle theory of leadership. *Training and Development Journal, 23,* 26–34.

Hope for urban education. (1999). Austin, TX: The Charles A. Dana Center, University of Texas at Austin.

House, R. J. (1971). A path-goal theory of leader effectiveness. *Administrative Science Quarterly, 16,* 321–328.

Jacobson, S. L., Brooks, S., Giles, C., Johnson, L., & Ylimaki, R. (2004). *Successful school leadership in high poverty schools: An examination of three urban elementary schools.* Buffalo, NY: Graduate School of Education, University of Buffalo.

Janis, I. L. (1972). *Victims of groupthink.* Boston: Houghton Mifflin.

Johnson, S. M. (2004). *Finders and keepers: Helping new teachers survive and thrive in our schools.* San Francisco: Jossey-Bass.

Johnson, S. M., Berg, J. H., & Donaldson, M. L. (2005). *Who stays in teaching and why: A review of the literature on teacher retention.* Cambridge, MA: Harvard Graduate School of Education, Project on the Next Generation of Teachers.

Kise, J. A. G., & Russell, B. (2008). *Differentiated school leadership: Effective collaboration, communication, and change through personality type.* Thousand Oaks, CA: Corwin.

Kozol, J. (1991). *Savage inequalities.* New York: Crown.

Leader, G. C. (2008). *Real leaders, Real schools.* Cambridge, MA: Harvard Education Press.

LeFloch, K. C., Martinez, F., O'Day, J., Stecher, B., Taylor, J., & Cook, A. (2007). *State and local implementation of the No Child Left Behind Act.* Volume III. Washington, DC: U.S. Department of Education, Office of Planning, Evaluation and Policy Development.

Leithwood, K., & Mascall, B. (2008). Collective leadership effects on student achievement. *Educational Administration Quarterly, 44*(4), 529–561.

Maehr, M. L., & Midgley, C. (1996). *Transforming school cultures.* Boulder, CO: Westview Press.

Manning, C., Sisserson, K., Jolliffe, D., Buenrostro, P., & Jackson, W. (2008). Professional evaluation as professional development. *Education and Urban Society, 40*(6), 715–729.

McKenzie, K. B., & Scheurich, J. J. (2004). Equity traps: A useful construct for preparing principals to lead schools that are successful with racially diverse students. *Educational Administration Quarterly, 40*(5), 601–632.

McLaughlin, M. W., Irby, M. A., & Langman, J. (1994). *Urban sanctuaries.* San Francisco: Jossey-Bass.

Meier, D. (1995). *The power of their ideas.* Boston: Beacon.

New Leaders for New Schools. (2008). Defining an urban principalship to drive dramatic achievement gains. Accessed from http://www.nlns.org

Northouse, P. G. (2007). *Leadership: Theory and practice* (4th ed.). Thousand Oaks, CA: Sage.

Oakes, J. (1985). *Keeping track: How schools structure inequality.* New Haven: Yale.

O'Day, J. (2002). Complexity, accountability, and school improvement. *Harvard Educational Review, 72*(3), 1–31.

Ogbu, J. U. (2003). *Black American students in an affluent suburb.* Mahwah, NJ: Erlbaum.

Ormrod, J. E. (1998). *Educational psychology* (2nd ed.). Columbus, OH: Merrill.

Payne, C. M. (2008). *So much reform, so little change.* Cambridge, MA: Harvard Education Press.

Picucci, A. C., Brownson, A., Kahlert, R., & Sobel, A. (2002). *Driven to succeed: High-performing, high-poverty turnaround middle schools.* Austin, TX: The Charles A. Dana Center, University of Texas.

Reeves, D. B. (2006). *The learning leader.* Alexandria, VA: Association for Supervision and Curriculum Development.

Rothstein, R. (2004). The achievement gap: A broader picture. *Educational Leadership, 62*(3), 40–43.

Sarason, S. B. (1982). *The culture of the school and the problem of change* (2nd ed.). Boston: Allyn & Bacon.

Schneider, B., & Stevenson, D. (1999). *The ambitious generation.* New Haven: Yale.

Slavin, R. E. (1998). Sand, bricks, and seeds: School change strategies and readiness for reform. In A. Hargreaves, A. Lieberman, M. Fullan, & D. Hopkins (eds.), *International handbook of educational change.* Dordrecht: Kluwer, 1299–1313.

Spillane, J. P. (2005). Distributed leadership. *The Educational Forum, 69,* 143–150.

Stiggins, R. (2007). Assessment through the student's eyes. *The Best of Educational Leadership: 2006–2007.* Alexandria, VA: Association for Supervision and Curriculum Development, 43–46.

Stone, D. (1989). Causal stories and the formation of policy agendas. *Political Science Quarterly, 104*(2), 281–300.

Stullich, S., Eisner, E., & McCrary, J. (2007). *National Assessment of Title I, final report: Volume I: Implementation.* Washington, DC: National Center for Education Evaluation, Institute for Education Sciences, U.S. Department of Education.

Toch, T. (2003). *High schools on a human scale.* Boston: Beacon.

Tyler, K. M., Uqdah, A. L., Dillihunt, R. B., Conner, T., Gadson, N., Henchy, A., et al. (2008). Cultural discontinuity: Toward a quantitative investigation of a major hypothesis in education. *Educational Researcher, 37*(5), 280–297.

Weinstein, R. S. (2002). *Reaching higher.* Cambridge, MA: Harvard University Press.

Woestehoff, J., & Neill, M. (2007). *Chicago school reform: Lessons for the nation.* Chicago: Parents United for Responsible Education.

Wright, W. E. (2007). A catch-22 for language learners. *The Best of Educational Leadership: 2006–2007.* Alexandria, VA: Association for Supervision and Curriculum Development, 14–18.

Index

CORWIN

A SAGE Company

The Corwin logo—a raven striding across an open book—represents the union of courage and learning. Corwin is committed to improving education for all learners by publishing books and other professional development resources for those serving the field of PreK–12 education. By providing practical, hands-on materials, Corwin continues to carry out the promise of its motto: **"Helping Educators Do Their Work Better."**